AFRICAN

FOUNDING E

PETER ABRAHAMS
  6 Mine Boy

CHINUA ACHEBE
  1 Things Fall Apart
  3 No Longer at Ease
  16 Arrow of God
  31 A Man of the People
  100 Girls at War*
  120 Beware Soul Brother†

TEWFIK AL-HAKIM
  117 Fate of a Cockroach‡

T. M. ALUKO
  11 One Man, One Matchet
  30 One Man, One Wife
  32 Kinsman and Foreman
  70 Chief, the Honourable
      Minister
  130 His Worshipful Majesty

ELECHI AMADI
  25 The Concubine
  44 The Great Ponds
  140 Sunset in Biafra§
  210 The Slave

JARED ANGIRA
  111 Silent Voices†

I. N. C. ANIEBO
  148 The Anonymity of Sacrifice
  206 The Journey Within

AYI KWEI ARMAH
  43 The Beautyful Ones Are
      Not Yet Born
  154 Fragments
  155 Why Are We So Blest?
  194 The Healers

BEDIAKO ASARE
  59 Rebel

KOFI AWOONOR
  108 This Earth, My Brother

FRANCIS BEBEY
  86 Agatha Moudio's Son
  205 The Ashanti Doll

MONGO BETI
  13 Mission to Kala
  77 King Lazarus
  88 The Poor Christ of Bomba
  181 Perpetua and the Habit of
      Unhappiness
  214 Remember Reuben

OKOT p'BITEK
  147 The Horn of My Love†
  193 Hare and Hornbill*

YAW M. BOATENG
  186 The Return

DENNIS BRUTUS
  46 Letters to Martha†
  115 A Simple Lust†
  208 Stubborn Hope†

AMILCAR CABRAL
  198 Speeches and Writing

Keys t
  Nove
  *Shor
  †Poetry
  ‡Plays
  §Autobiography or
    Biography

SYL CHENEY-COKER
  126 Concerto for an Exile†

DRISS CHRAIBI
  79 Heirs to the Past

J. P. CLARK
  50 America, Their America§

WILLIAM CONTON
  12 The African

BERNARD B. DADIE
  87 Climbié

DANIACHEW WORKU
  125 The Thirteenth Sun

MODIKWE DIKOBE
  124 The Marabi Dance

DAVID DIOP
  174 Hammer Blows†

MBELLA SONNE DIPOKO
  57 Because of Women
  82 A Few Nights and Days
  107 Black and White in Love†

AMU DJOLETO
  41 The Strange Man
  161 Money Galore

T. OBINKARAM ECHEWA
  168 The Land's Lord

CYPRIAN EKWENSI
  2 Burning Grass
  5 People of the City
  19 Lokotown*
  84 Beautiful Feathers
  146 Jagua Nana
  172 Restless City and
      Christmas Gold*
  185 Survive the Peace

OLAUDAH EQUIANO
  10 Equiano's Travels§

MALICK FALL
  144 The Wound

NURUDDIN FARAH
  80 From a Crooked Rib
  184 A Naked Needle

MUGO GATHERU
  20 Child of Two Worlds§

NADINE GORDIMER
  177 Some Monday for Sure*

JOE DE GRAFT
  166 Beneath the Jazz and
      Brass†

LUIS BERNARDO
HONWANA
  60 We Killed Mangy-Dog*

SONALLAH IBRAHIM
  95 The Smell of It*

YUSUF IDRIS
  209 The Cheapest Nights*

OBOTUNDE IJIMÈRE
  18 The Imprisonment of
      Obatala‡

EDDIE IROH
  189 Forty-Eight Guns for the
      General
  213 Toads of War

AUBREY KACHINGWE
  24 No Easy Task

SAMUEL KAHIGA
  158 The Girl from Abroad

CHEIKH HAMIDOU KANE
  119 Ambiguous Adventure

KENNETH KAUNDA
  4 Zambia Shall Be Free§

LEGSON KAYIRA
  162 The Detainee

A. W. KAYPER-MENSAH
  157 The Drummer in Our Time†

ASARE KONADU
  40 A Woman in her Prime
  55 Ordained by the Oracle

MAZISI KUNENE
  211 Emperor Shaka the Great

DURO LADIPO
  65 Three Yoruba Plays‡

ALEX LA GUMA
  35 A Walk in the Night*
  110 In the Fog of the Seasons'
      End
  152 The Stone Country
  212 The Time of the Butcherbird

DORIS LESSING
  131 The Grass is Singing

TABAN LO LIYONG
  69 Fixions*
  74 Eating Chiefs*
  90 Franz Fanon's Uneven Ribs†
  116 Another Nigger Dead†

BONNIE LUBEGA
  105 The Outcasts

YULISA AMADU MADDY
  89 Obasai‡
  137 No Past, No Present, No
      Future

151 *Midaq Alley*
197 *Miramar*

NELSON MANDELA
123 *No Easy Walk to Freedom*§

RENE MARAN
135 *Batouala*

DAMBUDZO MARECHERA
207 *The House of Hunger**

ALI A. MAZRUI
 97 *The Trial of Christopher
    Okigbo*

TOM MBOYA
 81 *The Challenge of
    Nationhood (Speeches)*

S. O. MEZU
113 *Behind the Rising Sun*

HAM MUKASA
133 *Sir Apolo Kagwa
    Discovers Britain*§

DOMINIC MULAISHO
 98 *The Tongue of the Dumb*
204 *The Smoke that Thunders*

CHARLES L. MUNGOSHI
170 *Waiting for the Rain*

JOHN MUNONYE
 21 *The Only Son*
 45 *Obi*
 94 *Oil Man of Obange*
121 *A Wreath for the Maidens*
153 *A Dancer of Fortune*
195 *Bridge to a Wedding*

MARTHA MVUNGI
159 *Three Solid Stones**

MEJA MWANGI
143 *Kill Me Quick*
145 *Carcase for Hounds*
176 *Going Down River Road*

GEORGE SIMEON MWASE
160 *Strike a Blow and Die*§

NGUGI WA THIONG'O
  7 *Weep Not Child*
 17 *The River Between*
 36 *A Grain of Wheat*
 51 *The Black Hermit*‡
150 *Secret Lives**
188 *Petals of Blood*
200 *Devil on the Cross*

NGUGI & MICERE MUGO
191 *The Trial of Dedan Kimathi*‡

REBEKA NJAU
203 *Ripples in the Pool*

ARTHUR NORTJE
141 *Dead Roots*†

NKEM NWANKWO
 67 *Danda*
173 *My Mercedes is Bigger
    Than Yours*

FLORA NWAPA
 26 *Efuru*
 56 *Idu*

ONUORA NZEKWU
 85 *Wand of Noble Wood*
 91 *Blade Among the Boys*

38 *Not Yet Uhuru*§

GABRIEL OKARA
 68 *The Voice*
183 *The Fisherman's
    Invocation*†

CHRISTOPHER OKIGBO
 62 *Labyrinths*†

KOLE OMOTOSO
102 *The Edifice*
122 *The Combat*

SEMBENE OUSMANE
 63 *God's Bits of Wood*
 92 *The Money-Order
    with White Genesis*
142 *Tribal Scars**
175 *Xala*

YAMBO OUOLOGUEM
 99 *Bound to Violence*

MARTIN OWUSU
138 *The Sudden Return*‡

FERDINAND OYONO
 29 *Houseboy*
 39 *The Old Man and the Medal*

PETER K. PALANGYO
 53 *Dying in the Sun*

SOL T. PLAATJE
201 *Mhudi*

R. L. PETENI
178 *Hill of Fools*

LENRIE PETERS
 22 *The Second Round*
 37 *Satellites*†
103 *Katchikali*†

**JEAN-JOSEPH
RABEARIVELO**
167 *Translations from the
    Night*†

MUKOTANI RUGYENDO
187 *The Barbed Wire &
    Other Plays*‡

MWANGI RUHENI
139 *The Future Leaders*
156 *The Minister's Daughter*

TAYEB SALIH
 47 *The Wedding of Zein**
 66 *Season of Migration to
    the North*

STANLAKE SAMKANGE
 33 *On Trial for my Country*
169 *The Mourned One*
190 *Year of the Uprising*

WILLIAMS SASSINE
199 *Wirriyamu*

KOBINA SEYKI
136 *The Blinkards*‡

SAHLE SELLASSIE
 52 *The Afersata*
163 *Warrior King*

FRANCIS SELORMEY
 27 *The Narrow Path*

71 *Nocturnes*†
180 *Prose and Poetry*

ROBERT SERUMAGA
 54 *Return to the Shadows*

WOLE SOYINKA
 76 *The Interpreters*

TCHICAYA U TAM'SI
 72 *Selected Poems*†

CAN THEMBA
104 *The Will to Die**

REMS NNA UMEASIEGBU
 61 *The Way We Lived**

LAWRENCE VAMBE
112 *An Ill-Fated People*§

J. L. VIEIRA
202 *The Real Life of Domingos
    Xavier*

D. M. ZWELONKE
128 *Robben Island*

**COLLECTIONS OF STORIES
AND PROSE**
  9 *Modern African Prose*
 14 *Quartet*
    By Richard Rive,
    Alex La Guma,
    Alf Wannenburgh and
    James Matthews
 15 *Origin East Africa*
 23 *The Origin of Life and Death*
 48 *Not Even God is Ripe
    Enough*
 58 *Political Spider*
 73 *North African Writing*
 75 *Myths and Legends of the
    Swahili*
 83 *Myths and Legends of the
    Congo*
109 *Onitsha Market Literature*
118 *Amadu's Bundle*
    Malum Amadu
132 *Two Centuries of African
    English*
196 *Egyptian Short Stories*

ANTHOLOGIES OF POETRY
  8 *A Book of African Verse*
 42 *Messages:
    Poems from Ghana*
 64 *Seven South African Poets*
 93 *A Choice of Flowers*
 96 *Poems from East Africa*
106 *French African Verse*
129 *Igbo Traditional Verse*
164 *Black Poets in South Africa*
171 *Poems of Black Africa*
192 *Anthology of Swahili Poetry*

COLLECTIONS OF PLAYS
 28 *Short East African Plays*
 34 *Ten One-Act Plays*
 78 *Short African Plays*
114 *Five African Plays*
127 *Nine African Plays for Radio*
134 *African Theatre*
165 *African Plays for Playing 1*
179 *African Plays for Playing 2*

Poems from East Africa

Edited by
David Cook
& David Rubadiri

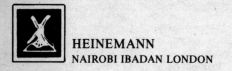

HEINEMANN
NAIROBI IBADAN LONDON

Heinemann Kenya Limited
Brick Court Mpaka Road / Woodvale Grove
P.O. Box 45314 Nairobi

in association with

Heinemann Educational Books
22 Bedford Square, London WC₁B 3HH
P.M.B. 5205 Ibadan.

ISBN 9966-46-019-5

Printed by
General Printers Ltd, Homa Bay Road,
P.O. Box 18001, Nairobi, Kenya.

CONTENTS

Acknowledgements   xi
Introduction   xiii

JARED ANGIRA   *Hunger*   1
                      Dialogue   2
                      No Coffin, No Grave   4
                      Primus Priory   6
                      The Siege of Ramogi   8
                      The Street   10

PETER ANYANG'-NYONG'O *Daughter of the Low
                       Land*   12

HENRY BARLOW   *Building the Nation*   14
                      *The Death of an
                       Eland*   16
                      *I Refuse to take your
                       Brotherly Hand*   18
                      The Village Well   20

RALPH BITAMAZIRE   *The Dog in Kivulu*   22
                      *I Love You, My
                       Gentle One*   23
                      *Putting Butter on a
                       Slice*   24
                      *Two Translations
                       from Rutooro*   26

A. S. BUKENYA   *I Met a Thief*   27
                      Whititude   28

[v]

CONTENTS

JOHN BUTLER *Kisenyi* 29

MURRAY CARLIN *Drummers at a Wrestling Match* 30
The Mango Tree 31

JIM CHAPLIN *The Next Morning* 32
Slum Day 33

A. R. CLIFF-LUBWA *The Beloved* 34

SAROJ DATTA *The Dead Bird* 35

SHEIKHA A. EL-MISKERY *The Crack* 36
Just a Word 37

LABAN ERAPU *An Elegy* 38
The Eyes That Wouldn't Wander 39
I Beg You 40
The Guilt of Giving 42
The Idol 43

DAVID GILL *The Expatriate* 44
Feud 45
The Mission 46
Swamp 47
Them and Us 48

CRISPIN HAULI *The Song of the Common Man* 49

CONTENTS

SABITI KABUSHENGA   *Saintless Still*   50
   Yet   54

WILLIAM KAMERA   *Poem in Four Parts*   60

JONATHAN KARIARA   *The Distance*   62
   Grass Will Grow   63
   *A Leopard Lives in
     a Muu Tree*   64
   Song   66
   Vietnam   67

JOSEPH KARIUKI   *Blind*   70
   Release   71
   Sleepless in Angola   72

AMIN KASSAM   *Martin Luther King*   73
   Mombasa   74
   Sunset   75
   Waiting for the Bus   76

YUSUF O. KASSAM   *Maji Maji*   77
   The Brewing Night   78
   Emptiness   80
   Ngoma   81
   *The Recurrent
     Design*   82
   The Splash   83

TABAN LO LIYONG   *the age of innocence
     is passed*   84
   *The Marriage of
     Black and White*   86

CONTENTS

	Gloria Bishop	88
	from: *Poems More*	90
	from: *Songs from the Congolese*	91
STEPHEN LUBEGA	*Evening*	92
	Requiem for Kagumba	93
JOHN S. MBITI	*The Crucified Thief*	94
	New York Skyscrapers	95
	My Father's Wooden House	96
	War After War	98
	Wearing Masks of Fear	99
ROSE MBOWA	*Ruin*	100
	That Game	101
ALEXANDER MUIGAI	*The Troubled Warrior*	102
PAUL MUKASA-SSALI	*Katebo Port*	104
	The Sentinel	105
	When You Come	106
MAGEMESO NAMUNGALU	*The Town Beauty*	107
	An Unlucky Lover	108
STELLA NGATHO	*Footpath*	109

CONTENTS

	The Kraal	110
	A Young Tree	111
VICTOR NGWABE	Makoha	112
RICHARD NTIRU	Modena	113
	The Pauper	114
	To the Living	116
	Virgine Madre	118
BENEDICT ONYANGO OGUTU	Voices of Transition	120
OKELLO OCULI	The Cross of Death	122
	The Return	123
OKOT P'BITEK	Return the Bridewealth	124
	They Sowed and Watered	130
OPINYA H. W. OKOTH-OGENDO	The Gambler	132
MARJORIE OLUDHE-MACGOYE	A Freedom Song	134
CHARLES OWUOR	I See a Road	136
DAVID RUBADIRI	Death at Mulago	137
	Paraa Lodge	138
	The Prostitute	139
	Two Epitaphs	140
	The Witch Tree at Mubende	142

CONTENTS

JOHN RUGANDA   *Barricades of Paper*
              Houses   143
              The Image of God   146

PROSCOVIA RWAKYAKA   *The Beard*   147
              The Inmates   148

NUWA SENTONGO   *Old Granny*   149
              The Pedestrian   150

JAGJIT SINGH   *Death etc., etc.*   152
              No Roots, No
              Leaves, No Buds   154
              Portrait of an Asian
              as an East African   156
              Public Butchery   160

JOHN SSEMUWANGA   *The Blind*   161
              Dual Piety   162
              Strange Breed   164

EVERETT STANDA   *I Speak for the*
              Bush   165

PARVIN SYAL   *The Pot*   167
              Defeat   168
              When I Came Here   170

MOHAMED TALIB   *The Corpse*   171
              Inanimate Sympathy   172

CONTENTS

BARRY TAYLOR *Dual Nationality* 173
I, Too 174

B. TEJANI *In the Orthopaedic
Ward* 175
On Top of Africa 176
*Wild Horse of
Serengeti* 178

HUBERT TEMBA *The Death of God* 180

EDWIN WAIYAKI *The Woman I
Married* 181

TIMOTHY WANGUSA *Kilembe Mines* 182
A Strange Wind 183
A Psalm of Lot 184
*A Taxi Driver on
his Death* 186

ACKNOWLEDGEMENTS

For permission to include the poems in this anthology acknowledgement is made to the following: Chatto & Windus, from *Men Without Evenings* by David Gill: 'The Expatriate', 'Feud', 'The Mission', 'Swamp', 'Them and Us'; The English Association, from *New Voices of the Commonwealth*, ed. Howard Sergeant: 'The Recurrent Design' by Yusuf O. Kassam, 'Dual Piety' by John Ssemuwanga, 'The Crack' by Sheikha A. El-Miskery, 'Ruin' by Rose Mbowa, 'The Beard' by Proscovia Rwakyaka, and 'A Strange Wind' by Timothy Wangusa.

A number of poems from this collection have been published in journals subsequent to agreement being reached on their inclusion in the present volume: *Transition*: 'Return the Bridewealth' by Okot p'Bitek, and 'Poem in Four Parts' by William Kamera; *Zuka* (Oxford University Press, E. Africa): 'Grass Will Grow', 'A Leopard Lives in a Muu Tree', and 'Song' by Jonathan Kariara, 'Evening' by Stephen Lubega, 'I See a Road' by Charles Owuor, and 'The Mango Tree' by Murray Carlin; *East Africa Journal*: 'The Dead Bird' by Saroj Datta, 'The Distance' by Jonathan Kariara, 'Blind', 'Release', and 'Sleepless in Angola' by Joseph Kariuki, 'The Cross of Death', and 'The Return' by Okello Oculi, 'A Freedom Song' by Marjorie Oludhe-Macgoye, 'The Prostitute', 'Paraa Lodge', and 'The Witch Tree at Mubende' by David Rubadiri, 'Death, etc., etc.,' and 'Public Butchery' by Jagjit Singh, 'I Speak for the Bush' by Everett Standa, 'The Woman I Married' by Edwin Waiyaki, 'Kilembe Mines' by Timothy Wangusa; *Nexus/Busara*: 'The Blind' by John Ssemuwanga, 'The Pot', and 'Defeat' by Parvin Syal, 'The Corpse', and 'Inanimate Sympathy' by

ACKNOWLEDGEMENTS

Mohamed Talib; *The Literary Review*: 'Slum Day' by Jim Chaplin, 'Image of God' by John Ruganda; *Prism*: 'The Beard' by Proscovia Rwakyaka, and 'A Taxi Driver on his Death' by Timothy Wangusa. *Penpoint*: 'Drummers at a Wrestling Match' by Murray Carlin, 'The Eyes that Wouldn't Wander', and 'The Guilt of Giving' by Laban Erapu, 'The Brewing Night', 'Emptiness', and 'The Recurrent Design' by Yusuf Kassam, 'Ruin', and 'That Game' by Rose Mbowa, 'Katebo Port' and 'The Sentinel' by Paul Mukasa-Ssali, 'The Inmates' by Proscovia Rwakyaka, 'The Pedestrian' by Nuwa Sentongo, 'Wild Horses of Serengeti' by B. Tejani, and 'A Strange Wind' by Timothy Wangusa.

INTRODUCTION

We are quite sure that critical comment would be out of place from the editors of a volume of new verse; and so in this introduction we shall restrict ourselves to explaining something of the scope and nature of this anthology.

We have attempted to assemble in this book a representative collection of poems written by East Africans, or written in East Africa by those involved in the literary scene, up to about Easter 1970. The only poems we have deliberately excluded from consideration are those which have already appeared in anthologies easily available in East Africa. Some fifteen of our chosen poems have been previously published in book form, and a few others are about to be so published; but these have either had extremely limited circulation locally, or are in collected writings by a single poet which may not for some time reach as wide a public as the writer might wish.

Another group of these poems will be familiar to some readers from the pages of *Transition*, *Ghala* and *Zuka*. These are now presented in a more permanent form. Poems which have appeared in books or in the journals just named form about a third of the collection. In many cases, probably the majority, these poems now appear in revised versions which the authors regard as final. On the other hand, Okot p'Bitek's 'They Sowed and Watered' has, since we chose it, been transmuted into a section of *Song of Ocol*: no doubt many readers will be interested to compare the two quite different arrangements.

Another third part of this collection has been brought together from various student publications in East Africa; though these writings have always been selected from a full range of manuscripts submitted by each poet, and have often gone through a sea-change since their trial appearances. And the remaining third of the poems we have chosen have not so far, to the best of our knowledge, enjoyed even a limited circulation in print.

It has not always been easy to make or keep contact with half a hundred poets: our correspondence has ranged from Canada to India. One or two writers have preferred not to appear in this collection. In the case of six poems we have simply to reprint the version that we found published elsewhere; but in every other instance we have been in direct touch with the writers and feel confident that we have been able to produce precisely the poet's final decision on wording and punctuation.

The biographical notes are taken from data provided by the writers themselves.

Editing can seem a thankless task; and the editing of poetry may at times appear particularly paradoxical. But in spite of our moments of self-doubt or frustration, we have both been gratified as well as humbled by our responsibilities. Our contributors have been very co-operative. It is difficult to love an editor: but we have met with remarkable understanding and (even at the worst) forbearance. We have read hundreds of poems and we owe much to the many promising writers whose works we have not been able to include. When we started we were quite prepared to limit ourselves to a smaller collection than this has turned out to be: indeed it is slightly larger in the event than the upper limits originally proposed by our publishers. This is because we found more poems that we think to be good than we had expected.

The maize will grow
once when
long rains have come
and army worms
have gone

rations
will sink
with hunger
and the coiled intestines
will straighten

But

that day
shall find many
in the invalid home
with collar'd fathers
at bedside mass
and others
in graves
with maggots
on palatable meal

and for the grave majesties
the maize cob
shall be
for a rusty funeral feast.

O Lord Make Haste to Help Me
O Man Make Haste to Repent

O Padre open the Vestroom
O Man Confess Your Sins

O Father I have no Sins
O Man You Are Not Ready

> Pulpit abandoned
> The weight of celibacy

> Collection dish empty
> Poverty of churchgoers

> Kneelers and tendants
> Satiety in sins

O Lord Make Haste to Save us
O Man You Are Not Hungry

> Lord will you Hear Our Cry
> About this World With End

Man I will hear your Cry
About this World Without End

O Lord Shall We Communicate
O Man I am God Almighty

O Lord Will You hear my request
O Man about my kingdom

[2]

O Lord Its all about My adultrous Wife
               about My bills
               about My demotion
               about My failure
               about all these
               World With End

O Man about all these
               See Your reverend Priest
               See Your Comrade Fortune
               See Your Comate Nature

O Lord Let My Cry Come Unto You
O Man Do you hear my Sermon?

O Lord Cannot I see your face

O Man empathy is mine, sympathy is yours,
O Man You'll never see My Face

O Lord Then You Are Not of Mercy of Grace!

He was buried without a coffin
without a grave
the scavengers performed the post-mortem
in the open mortuary
without sterilized knives
in front of the night club

stuttering rifles staged
the gun salute of the day
that was a state burial
the car knelt
the red plate wept, wrapped itself into its master's blood

his diary revealed to the sea
the rain anchored there at last
isn't our flag red, black and white?
so he wrapped himself well

who could signal yellow
when we had to leave politics to the experts
and brood on books
brood on hunger
and schoolgirls
grumble under the black pot
sleep under torn mosquito net
and let lice lick our intestines
the lord of the bar, money speaks madam
woman magnet, money speaks madam
we only cover the stinking darkness
of the cave of our mouths
and ask our father who is in hell to judge
the quick and the good

[4]

well, his diary, submarine of the Third World War
showed he wished
to be buried in a gold-laden coffin
like a VIP
under the jacaranda tree beside his palace
a shelter for his grave
and much beer for the funeral party

anyway one noisy pupil suggested we bring
tractors and plough the land.

My man is gone away to serve
                         the Master
                         his chief
At the set of the sun
                         the pigeons
                         and wagtails
                         are homing
Lurking along the cold side
The black wall of euphorbia
                         concrete
Down the valley I hear
                         the shepherds call
The Wolves have howled
                         from the hillside
                         caves
The half-potent old men
                         virility sailed away with time
                         Minutes turned into years
The worn-out old men
                         sing rustless epics
                         from beer-party gospels:
                         The golden flutes
I do not know, I do not know
I cannot tell, And I cannot tell
                         When my Man will come
                         When my Man will come
I must live these days alone
For my man must serve the Chief
The weaverbird should rest in her nest
And stir not the heat-burnt hope
For the fog is still absent

[6]

Let peasants cry into the dusk
The fields have partial answers
Children endlessly rock in the cradles
Shall I go to find My Mate?
Hunger shall never let me rest
The hours delve into years
Soon I shall have no tears to shed
No laughter to burst
I will not know
When first it started.

That chloroform sleep
woke me up
in dream
only to find
Ramogi under siege

the calabash lay
in the fireplace
where the fire
had burnt it half
and the fire itself
had gone out half

the half dead tree
on the river bank
lay growing
on the ground

the fire had sunk
below the granary
and the eggs
long hidden there
were in hatching
by that heat.

I saw the drum
hanged on a siala tree
and 'osimbo'
in a potato field

[8]

Ramogi stood unstirred
on the lakeshore
watching waves
watching diving fishermen
raise and sink their heads
and a spoilt son
played the guitar
the harp lay idle
near the 'duol'

The fishes cried
and the crocodiles slept
beneath the feet
of Ramogi
who cast a look
at the yonder bank
and saw
The Nilus flow.

Worms crawling   Worms crawling
            mercedes slides past
                blue shadow

                    garbage

        swinging   swinging
        boozing   boozing

            zephyr slides past
            green shadow

                garbage
            black shadow

    Wananchi   Wananchi

                scratch
                scratch
                tiny nails
            blocked nostrils

vultures whirr   vultures whirr

            The band splashes
            up the night-club

                rolls royce
                sleek and cool
                grey shadow

                fireworks
                diwali
                warning light

by shops   by shops

'closing down sale'
non-citizen
gloom   shadow

mercedes
trinity   mansion   trinity
shamba

and the street is clean
the street is clean

PETER ANYANG'-NYONG'O *Daughter of the Low Land*

After I have communed with them,
With dead men's ideas;
'Nya dyang'' comes to me
With accusing persuasion:
         'Come, "wuod twon",
         My activities are vital.'

I do not let my testicles
Be crushed when I am wide awake
By the ghosts of an alien clan
In the half-lighted book-cave;
No!
When I sheathe the family spear
And unfeather the poison-horned arrow;
When I expose the daughter of the low land
To village gossip and contempt;
Then the books that I read
Smash my testicles in my sleep!

My testicles
Have not been smashed
By heavy books!
         'Ocol,
         Drink from the roots;
         You were first wedded to me
         And then to Plato
         And Aristotle.'

I do not sit there
In that forest
Of dead men's heads

[12]

Letting their heavy tongues –
Like 'rungus' –
Butt my balls to wind's dust;
No!
Like the emissary
Of a semi-famished land,
Or the scout of a belligerent army,
I brew with the enemy
And drink with my people.

And when I return home
To the daughter of the brave one,
The yeast from the low land
Makes my manhood
Rise.

Today I did my share
In building the nation.
I drove a Permanent Secretary
To an important urgent function
In fact to a luncheon at the Vic.

The menu reflected its importance
Cold Bell beer with small talk,
Then fried chicken with niceties
Wine to fill the hollowness of the laughs
Ice-cream to cover the stereotype jokes
Coffee to keep the PS awake on return journey.

I drove the Permanent Secretary back.
He yawned many times in back of the car
Then to keep awake, he suddenly asked,
Did you have any lunch friend?
I replied looking straight ahead
And secretly smiling at his belated concern
That I had not, but was slimming!

Upon which he said with a seriousness
That amused more than annoyed me,
Mwananchi, I too had none!
I attended to matters of state.
Highly delicate diplomatic duties you know,
And friend, it goes against my grain,
Causes me stomach ulcers and wind.
Ah, he continued, yawning again,
The pains we suffer in building the nation!

So the PS had ulcers too!
My ulcers I think are equally painful
Only they are caused by hunger,
Not sumptuous lunches!

So two nation builders
Arrived home this evening
With terrible stomach pains
The result of building the nation —
– Different ways.

Those eyes!
Those liquid green eyes
Tearless yet crying
Terrified and silent
Imploring for mercy
Those eyes haunt me.

We stood and looked at her
Emaciated with hunger and pain
Lying on her side with the festering leg
Dripping with pus held in the air
Trying in vain to heave itself up with her other legs.

Those eyes!
The terrified liquid eyes
Fervently transmitted pleas for Mercy
And the body shook with terror and pain
The emaciated legs kicked feebly
Trying to get her up
Where she had tripped and fallen.
There were ticks on her belly
Some were fat and bluish green
And there were numerous small brown ones.
The eyes begged!
Those haunting eyes.

The hunter said in a matter of fact way
It is kinder to shoot her
And raised his gun.
There was a kick and a feeble neigh
The body relaxed; the neck fell back.
The eyes looked at me
Still pleading
As if the hunter had not been merciful
And I stood there
Feeling foolish
I noticed the ticks –
Still sucking.
I walked away
With liquid eyes
And followed the hunter.

Your nails are black with dirt, brother
And your palms are clammy with sweat
I refuse to take the hand you extend in help
I shall not join hands with you brother
For unclean hands make me uneasy
For filthy fingernails rob me of my pride.

You argue, gesticulating with your once
Impeccably clean and beautiful hands
That before long it shall not matter
For 'everybody' is delving and digging
And all shall have hands dripping with dirt.

That nobody shall know what clean hands look like
And there shall be comfort in the dirty crowd
And enough to eat, for there are good yields
When the stinking manure is well dug in
With strong and bold hands in time.

Are you going blind brother?
I ask how many have the sludge
Or the strong and bold hands like yours
With which to dig and delve?
Brother the hands of many are too weak with hunger
And for many the sludge is out of reach
And yet for others the stink is too nauseating!
But all have eyes and hunger fills them with anger
As they watch your fingernails fill with dirt!

I have seen hungry envious eyes
Watching silently through your chain-link fence
I have seen eyes in deep sunken sockets
Burning with anger intently watching you
I have seen parched mouths water with saliva
And heard the rumbling of hollow empty stomachs
As they watched you feed the dog with meat
From the heavy yields of the city sludge.

Have you entirely forgotten Brother
The fragrance and comfort of clean hands?
The confidence, the peace you have when you know
You'll leave no ugly smudge upon the sheet?
Don't you remember the repulsion you had
When you shook hands with fat dirty men
With their dirty clammy palms?

Let me alone Brother and from the top of the cliff
Don't offer me your dirty hand in help.
Let me trudge the long way up
For the short cuts are soiled and slippery
Your palms are clammy with the sweat of fear
And your fingernails are clogged with dirt.

By this well,
Where fresh waters still quietly whisper
As when I
First accompanied Mother and filled my baby gourd,
By this well,
Where many an evening its clean water cleaned me;

This silent well
Dreaded haunt of the long haired Musambwa,
Who basked
In the mid-day sun reclining on the rock
Where I now sit
Welling up with many poignant memories;

This spot,
Which has rung with the purity of child laughter;
This spot,
Where eye spoke secretly to responding eye;
This spot,
Where hearts pounded madly in many a breast;

By this well,
Over-hung by leafy branches of sheltering trees
I first noticed her.
I saw her in the cool of a red, red evening.
I saw her
As if I had not seen her a thousand times before.

By this well
My eyes asked for love, and my heart went mad.
I stuttered.
And murmured my first words of love
And cupped,
With my hands, the intoxication that were her breasts.

In this well,
In the clear waters of this whispering well,
The silent moon
Witnessed with a smile our inviolate vows,
The kisses
That left us weak and breathless.

It is dark.
It is dark by the well that still whispers.
It is darker,
It is utter darkness in the heart that bleeds
By this well,
Where magic has evaporated but memories linger.

Of damp death
The rotting foliage reeks,
And the branches
Are grotesque talons of hungry vultures,
For she is dead.
The one I first loved by this well.

The dog in Kivulu,
Thin, bony and yawning;
The dog in Kivulu,
Panting and squatting
Like its master.
The dog in Kivulu,
Barking at naked children,
Children who sing a thanksgiving
As they leave the rubbish heaps.
The dog in Kivulu,
Running away from fat flies
And scratching its tail with teeth,
Biting nothing but its own gums,
Swallowing nothing more than its own saliva.
The dog of Kivulu,
Guarding its drunkard master
And the hoard of fermenting millet,
Kwete and malwa in clay-pots.
But the dog of Kivulu
Lies by, with nothing to drink;
Nobody calls it Acaali, the bitch,
It looks on – at the trenches –
And drinks the water from the cattleshed.

I love you, my gentle one;
My love is the fresh milk in the rubindi
Which you drank on the wedding day;
My love is the butter we were smeared with
To seal fidelity into our hearts.
You are the cattle-bird's egg,
For those who saw you are wealthy;
You are the papyrus reed of the lake,
Which they pull out with both hands.
And I sing for you with tears
Because you possess my heart:
I love you, my gentle one.

Putting butter on a slice, and in the pan rice,
Wiping sweat with a towel, that is the world now,
Opening a Nile with an opener, drinking and talking,
Lifting the telephone and signing a cheque,
Drafting and glancing to check,
Hello and how are you, every morning
      Planning – for the week-end,
To have a step with Joy and keep the legs moving,
A ride to the botanical gardens,
At Three Stars or Gardenier tonight we dine,
Playing records on the jukebox,
A sleepless night, without breakfast,
Waking rolled up on the Vono.
      Putting butter on a slice, that is the world now.
What is Bazaarrabusa saying and meaning,
'The-one-with-love-that-echoed-mine',
Can I write a line like this?
Oh, I have no time for poetry:
Its world is Mars;
I will read and write it on computers.
      This is Eden, pressing buttons to move,
With no need to think, only look at the moon,
No more need to write for Eden is Heaven,
Turning the tap and off glides the soot,
The mind abounds in love and fruit,
The power to read and to write works of art,
Has melted to Eden from the heart.
      Putting butter on a slice,
That is the world now.

What better heaven is there,
When body and mind are wholly in Eden
Putting butter on a slice;
Eden is Heaven,
Where works of art are no more.

I

Hear, hear this my poem
Those who do not have any
                    Take mine,
Hear this thunder of victory
                    The song of my ancestors:
Short men I fling like stones,
Tall ones I cut like sorghum;
My mother sent me for water
I brought her clots of blood,
My father sent me for firewood
I brought him bundles of broken spears.
And they called me twin-father
When in fact I never produced any,
I produced them only with Nyamucikinya
                    my small Spear,
                    my poem.

II

I love you my Lord
When I see you sigh,
I love you my Lord
When I see your lion stature I pant.
You charmed me:
You charmed me with the 'Earth's Laughter'
When I see you I laugh alone;
You charmed with the 'Earth's joke',
When I see you, I play about;
When you are not near
My body itches;
I love you my Lord.

[26]

On the beach, on the coast,
Under the idle, whispering coconut towers,
Before the growling, foaming, waves,
I met a thief, who guessed I had
An innocent heart for her to steal.

She took my hand and led me under
The intimate cashew boughs which shaded
The downy grass and peeping weeds.
She jumped and plucked the nuts for me to suck;
She sang and laughed and pressed close.

I gazed: her hair was like the wool of a mountain sheep,
Her eyes, a pair of brown-black beans floating in milk.
Juicy and round as plantain shoots
Her legs, arms and neck;
And like wine-gourds her pillowy breasts;
Her throat uttered fresh banana juice:
Matching her face – smooth and banana-ripe.

I touched – but long before I even tasted,
My heart had flowed from me into her breast;
And then she went – High and South –
And left my carcase roasting in the fire she'd lit.

A. S. BUKENYA *Whititude*

I envied his being Negro:
For there he was with his hardened face
That told of night and her mystery,
Of age and varied experience.
In shame, in fear, in joy, his hue the same,
Unlike my baby skin that told of all I felt.
And while I pitied him for being black,
I feared he had a depth unknown to me,
Which his darkness hid.

JOHN BUTLER *Kisenyi*

Let us not lie to ourselves.
A skeleton is skeleton
Whether hot, white under the sun
Or metamorphosed by the mystery
Of African African moon.

Let us not look either
At this frantic place
Only with beastly eyes
Of sanitary squads.
Do not see only
Mud and mabati
Baziba and Swahili.
For lip-locked, twain and twain
In so secret darkness
Sacredly, compulsively
Perform the rite.
Truly here is compulsion
That is very heart.

Some urgency imprisoned among the drums
Is never discharged; that bending energy
Is its own end, that tune is a deep confusion
Not in itself confused, not in its core:
There, there beats a vision of the old wars
Where the short panting of the gourds shaken
The shifting voice of the battle, the confusion of decision,
The drastic authority of the tenor drum
Leading them away, imposing a sudden order
New, yet old, make quarrelsome unison.

The drums are like men shouting with open mouths
On some continuous furious frieze of campaign:

So loud they are, their noise is a kind of silence.

Men of the milder zone, you find
   Are used to the beauties of summer space
   Their tall trees cast their scent
For miles, the air being warm, the wind

Steady, and blossoms in the sky . . .
   But where the drop drops with a report
   Upon the leaf; where the curled
Bark and the sticks begin to fly

Where the storms surging strain
   To bend the big tops, and the flash
   Lights every leaf, and men must race
The roaring myriads of the rain

That depth of hollow must and dead
   Darkness under the mango tree
   Gives shelter; it will lighten to
A green hall once the rains have fled

Approaching it, you may be afraid
   As, in its equatorial
   Glitter, tick and hum, it stands
Rounded, having an enormous shade

There is a rustling floor there
   It will carry its own seasons
   Full green, fresh green, rust
These can be seen throughout the year

Small blossom. Boys heave a stone
   In the infathomable green
   Or bring, weighing on the great bough
Its fibrous sweet birth down.

[31]

Was this where I came staggering?
This the inviting portal to delight:
Three box-lids and a half-peeled log.

Was this the hall that opened wide?
Promising soft richness of desire:
Two army blankets hung on a knotted string.

Was this she who called me in?
She of seductive grace beyond the others:
Grasping, blowsed with our soft caressing.

Was that the man who came inside?
That peeling reflection of beer-shot eyes:
That pocketless, drained, dejected, I.

The monotonous tap of the blacksmiths' sounds.
Long shadows zebra the roads;
Partners stretch and yawn,
Their girls catch up on sleep.
Dew lies still on the piled maize,
And children tumble their way to school.

The vendors squat behind their wares.
Careful spenders have enough for food,
The careless flounder in the shade
Press emptiness against worn grass.
The pious wash and pray.
Heat stills the birds: the crickets sing.

Smoke curls to stifle the quiet air.
The lamps are lit: music begins to play.
As bars begin to fill,
The girls waken and parade.
Children quarrel their way to bed.
Life has been won from another day.

Lapobo,
Tall but not too tall,
Short but not too short,
She is of medium size.

Lapobo,
Her teeth are not as ash
Nor the colour of maize flour,
Her teeth are white as fresh milk.
The whiteness of her teeth
When I think of her
Makes food drop from my hand.

Lapobo,
Black but not too black,
Brown but not too brown,
Her skin colour is just between black and brown.

Lapobo,
Her heels have no cracks,
Her palms are smooth and tender to touch,
Her eyes – Ho they can destroy anybody.

SAROJ DATTA *The Dead Bird*

Dead on my palm
A slab of silent meat
Suspended between stiffness and rotting
Bones sitting stolid on my skin
The beak clamped tight
Unsoftened by the feathers
A final refusal
Hanging determined from the weak neck
Eyes bright with liquid
Desperate with concentrated feeling
Smouldering into me
The sun's lens-captured heat finding a point to scorch
The curling feathers, screams,
Imprisoning the whole world's silences
Recoiling from my foreign breath
Pink skin drily accepting feather ends
Rustling cage of feathers
Flapping and raging in my mind
Would never float wind-lightened
Empty itself of song
Because a pump refused to beat
An eternity of grace
Cradled and responsive in my hand.

SHEIKHA A. EL-MISKERY *The Crack*

Crack the glass,
And the crack
Will always remain.
The human heart
Has the same vein;
It's just as delicate
To the strain.

Once it is hurt,
It is too hard
To fade the stain.
Though parts can
Fix together –
You've just to touch the wound,
To make it drain again.

When dogs encounter
They hesitate,
They sense a kinship
Stop, sniff, then part.

As birds glide they tune
A mutual note,
Beak to beak greetings flare
To form the music of the air.

Even cups in a tray
Make a sound as they touch;
Leaves rustle;
Yet the human voice is hushed.

Strangers silently we passed
Only to look behind:
The other's head has also turned
As if to greet my mind.

When he was here,
We planned each tomorrow
With him in mind
For we saw no parting
Looming beyond the horizon.

When he was here,
We joked and laughed together
And no fleeting shadow of a ghost
Ever crossed our paths.

Day by day we lived
On this side of the mist
And there was never a sign
That his hours were running fast.

When he was gone,
Through glazed eyes we searched
Beyond the mist and the shadows
For we couldn't believe he was nowhere:
We couldn't believe he was dead.

Yours were the eyes that wouldn't wander,
We met and parted like strangers,
Strangers who would not forget
But met again and again
As if by chance,
Bypassing each other and smiling
As though to someone else.

What was it that led us
Somewhere beyond
The eyes of the crowd
To a lonely spot
Where the eyes that wouldn't wander
Slowly rose and looked into mine?
What was this feeling
That raptured my nerves
As your trim fingers
Linked with mine?
What power lay hidden
In those eyes
That wouldn't wander?

I beg you,
If you feel something like love for me,
Not to let me know it now
When I feel nothing so certain for you –
Wait until you've conquered my pride
By pretending not to care for me.

I beg you,
If you think your eyes will give you away,
Not to give me that longing look
When you know it will force the moment –
Wait until our heartbeats have settled
Then put your head on my shoulder.

I beg you
Not to let us surrender to passion
Until our liking has grown to love:
Let's stop and look back,
Let's draw apart and sigh,
Let's stand back to back,
Let's say good-bye for the day
And walk our different ways
Without pausing to wait
For an echo to our last word.

I beg you,
If you find yourself interlocked
In my embrace,
To kiss me and keep me silent
Before I start making promises
That time may choose to byepass –

[40]

Wait until our hands are free,
Then listen to me;
Wait until our love is primed,
Then give me your hand.

You've seen that heap of rags
That pollutes the airconditioned
City Centre,
That louse that creeps about
In the clean core of sophistication;
You've seen him waylay his betters
And make them start –
Especially when they have no change.

You recall the day you came upon him
And were startled by his silent presence
Intruding into your preoccupation:
You hurled a coin
Which missed the mark
And rolled into the gutter
Where he groped for it
With a chilling grotesque gratitude
That followed you down the street.
You dived into the nearest shop
To escape the stare
Of the scandalised crowd
That found you guilty
Of recalling attention
To the impenetrable patience
They had learnt not to see.

Brown, proud and flawless,
Wordless and passionless,
You stand on the shelf,
On the pedestal I built for you –
An idol in a Christian house.

Curved, polished and oiled,
Primed and perfect,
You came to my life
A goddess to whom I offer
My first and my last prayer.

Serene and silent
You stand on your pedestal,
Aloof and alone,
Too high above the tears I shed
For the love that was not,
Too far beyond the reach of arms
That rise in mute prayer
And beg to be released
From the hold
Of eyes to blind for tears
And a heart too stern
For pity.

DAVID GILL *The Expatriate*

Here I sit with every mortal gadget round me.
Klemperer conducts from his narrow groove
and Brahms breaks like a sea against the windows –
an imposing European noise.
Or, if I wish, the radio with its sorcery of wires and valves
will fill this room with tongues and tragedy.
Or when a glinting bird alights in view of these tall
    windows,
I snatch my violet-tinted, smooth-adjusting binoculars
to see more definitely.
These things, my adjuncts, live with me, belong these
    Siebensachen
like Jupiter's old moons to Jupiter – and yet
I'm only conscious of their modern presence when
that boy appears
that small black boy that stands
so shyly at the window looking in
through sad soft eyes
like two dark holes
in a forest-wall.

After the parents have gone to burn the houses of the
    parents below
and those below in turn have burnt the houses of those
    above
who started the burnings,
the children of the mountains, who were hidden but saw,
are shelled by the dawn from their pod of darkness
and creep dry-eyed to the ring of homely embers
and stare at what half-charred remains there are:
a blackened stool, a cooking pot, some tins.

And then the unhabitual silence swells all intervals,
no cocks are crowing, goats all gone.
With desolate eyes they stare across the valley
as the long sealed trains of cloud slide past
deporting their fathers and mothers . . .

For sixty years or more the mission church
has let the lanterns of its chalk-white walls
so shine before the shouting mountain men
that some slight shift of soul may well
be posited.

The sabbath drums boom out their routine summons
among the candled coral trees – and down
the mountain's grassy runnels tribesmen pour
to worship and the whitewashed walls resound
with battered diatonic hymns.

The preacher preaches love: love one another.
(How can we love the plainsmen when they burn
our houses, steal our goats and rape our wives?
We'll love all men as Master Jesus did
except the lowlanders.)

On Monday morn the curling fleece of smoke
dilates above the plainsmen's huts. And down
crash axed banana trees. And leg-trussed goats
stagger and scream. Above the bedlam hangs
the white star of persistent Christ.

DAVID GILL *Swamp*

Dry-season dust-tails dogged the cars along
the orange tracks when we began to curb
the croaking swamp. Stripped schoolboys hacked
the ankles of the giant reeds. A song

rose somewhere as the rippling line advanced,
disgruntled mostly, swiping with Birmingham bush-knives
and curling sickles. Few really grasped the idea
that civilized man will not endure a swamp.

Still seeing little sense in what they did,
they burnt the grass and dug some crooked drains.
White blooms of smoke grew huge above the swamp
at dusk and exiled all the frogs' refrains.

Rough places smooth, O make! Use hand and hoe!
Control the lie of land and guide the flow
of rain. Be conquerors subduing all:
my own philosophy runs roughly so.

We cleared the thistles and the reeds, we dug
our ditches deep; then came the spearing rain.
And now the fatalists can smirk and say:
Look, sir, the grasses have grown tall again.

They are rooted here. Their tenuous life,
haunted by ancestors, walks beneath these leaves.
Out of sight but always well in earshot
our neighbours weave the slow grass mats
of their dark-green unfathomable lives,

whilst we in our dry, well-furnished houses
(the Protectorate served its servants well)
with house-boys polishing the spacious acres,
stare out across the smooth manorial lawns
and red platoons of cannas through the trees
to alien hills that shoulder us away.

They drive me along,
        they do they do,
These my brothers no longer brothers –
Their hands are whips, along they drive me,
No longer am I the same mother's child.

They push me along,
        indeed they do,
These my sisters no longer sisters –
Their mouths are cannons, spittle of fire,
No longer am I the same father's pride.

They kick me along,
        they do they do,
These my playmates no longer playmates –
Their actions are fates, my life they decide,
No longer am I the same free-born human.

They abuse me,
        they do time and again,
Fellow humans load me with all their bundles –
They are my masters, and me a poor ass,
To be driven, pushed, kicked and abused.

I

We lived long time ago
Owners of these hollow droning voices.
To the remnants of that world
Belong our haggard looks
Our drilling long stares
Our motionless bodies
Once, awakening to come up,
Smiling,
Smiling because we understand
We understand well,
We are only disfigured relics
Shaking from fossil extinctions,
Emerging.

Mountain rocks gape in jagged yawns,
Winds blow,
Hot air.
We evolve
Evolving
Stuffed images of prehistory
Blending slowly into the march.

None asks for our names
Nobody knows we are here.
Those who gaze
Shift away
Bending their brows
Evasive,
Unsure how to greet us.

[50]

II

We stand expectant,
Naked stones
Hugging ribs with the dust from the pub
Hoping one, amazed, may repeat:
We know these faces;
In the long past,
We saw these faces somewhere,
But God,
We do not remember,
We cannot remember these men,
But they do,
Looking through ashamed recognition.
See how they smile,
One says,
Let us stand them a pint
Another one shakes his head,
No.
Visions do not,
Oh no.
Visions don't.
But we know we lived long time ago
We only smile
Ghastly.
Also recall,
They are impatient men
The longing men
With days to number
Hours to save
Minutes to hurry.

III

When evening breezes stir again,
Mountains conspire with nights
Trees hustle us back
Along narrowing paths of lost recollection
We pace up
Hurried steps
Fleeing the humdrum
Escaping our humdrum.

Our doors locked
Rooms harbour unbelievable servants
We chew our surviving dregs of the day
We think of tomorrow.
The day,
The hypnotic rays of the day,
An exile from our intimates.
We smile,
Again.
Good Lord
Again,
The men we shall see
The words we shall say.

We remember,
Natives of a deserted camp
Moving naked in somnolence
Thinking only of the noon,
Alive with a sickness to the drying wells.
Men without trust in fortunes
Yet look askance at a buzzing fly.
The same men

[52]

Who feel the draining day
And swallow to appease their thirst-crazed throats
Men who spit in dust
Evading their sweat with a greasy palm.
Perhaps somewhere
Another is sighing:
It is the only substance.

IV

We cross fingers
Renouncing our past curses
We covet another drink
Sleeping
Forgetting
Our duties
Our rights
Nobody gives us any
We regret none.

Only stinging winds
Hot stinging winds of sand
Desolate scrubby trees
And looming mountains
There, and the naked men,
Stick hard on our palates
Reminding us we are still here
Perhaps still holding on,
Clutching on the crest of a receding world
Waiting, patient
Ready to flare a good-bye
A farewell
Before we silently wither.

Mr Gwentamu submits
Deciding
Mrs Gwentamu persists
Insisting
You can't say I did it
No, dear
Oh, dear
Then
Dear
You can't say I did it
Did it, dear?
Though, my dear
What, dear?
You don't know
I don't know
My dear
You can't know
And that's the point
That's the point
I see
Of course you don't
I mean
You don't see
The point
Why
You can't see
Dear
I can't see?

You can't really look and see
I see
You don't
That's the point
That's the point
The whole damned point
The reason
Why
You don't
Look at me
Or at you
About you
About me
About us
You can't see
No you can't
You can't
You really can't
You can't possibly do
See
Me
You
Why?
I don't know
And that's the point
Get the book
It doesn't see
But you read

Read
Yes read
Read to know
To know
Know
The point
What point?
I see
But you don't
When I do
Let us then
Go on
Go on
I know
Go on
And get off
I don't know
And that's the point
You said
There's no point
Because
We
We
You and me
Both of us
Know
That
You know

You said
I didn't say
You did
You don't have to
Know
Who says
What.
Everybody
All of them
The whole lot
Know
Every one
Why
They don't
Don't speak
You see
I see
Nobody knows
The whole damned thing
You see
I don't want
To know
Why
They say
It doesn't matter
It doesn't matter
Forget it
Forget it

Never mind
Mind
Nothing
What is nothing
Forget it
Forget it
Forget
Everything
Well
Damn it
Forget
Forget
Okay
Kiss me
I love you
You love me
Let us go
I am ready
Things off
And
I love you
Very much
Okay
That's all
What
Everything
Yes,
God

What
I am frozen
Hell
You can't say I did it
Oh, dear
You can't say I did it

I

The leaves are withered
Roses fold and shrink.
Dog, the panting athlete, shows his tongue.
A dwarfed shadow flees –
Hides under my legs
Nuts wrinkle and crack.

II

The sun is old
The west glows like a worm
Shadows are long
There are cool whispers in the trees
The weavers make for their homes
Old Kibo in his 'kanga' appears.

III

Like honey you covered the lawn
    Fleeting beauty –
In the cool of the morning air
Peace-placid and pleasant.

The moist crystals of yesternight
    Where are you gone?
I would have you for my own.
Surrendered at the approach of dawn.

IV

Sun from his eastern cradle
Like a chameleon measures his steps
Stretches his tender arms
Over the silent hills.
The trees exchange greetings
In the gentle whispers of dawn.
The lazy night is over.

The weaverbird disturbs my rest.
Day hatching from the eastern shell
Uncovers ice-shouldered Kibo.
Life blooms with the rose
In the cool of the morning air
The lazy night is over.

The distance we've travelled together
  is short
A maid may easily do it.

We've travelled together
We
                        plunged in
Where a maid would only have wetted her toes.

Crossed continents in boats that leaked
Our hands darted frantically as we
Moulded the clay to stop
The gaps –
And became ONE.

From you I took fire
My pots would have lain cracked
Abandoned in the sun.

Now I tap them delicately
Fearing their silent completeness.
It's you I hear
Rich and Resonant.

JONATHAN KARIARA *Grass Will Grow*

If you should take my child Lord
Give my hands strength to dig his grave
Cover him with earth
Lord send a little rain
For grass will grow.

If my house should burn down
So that the ashes sting the nostrils
Making the eyes weep
Then Lord send a little rain
For grass will grow.

But Lord do not send me
Madness
I ask for tears
Do not send me moon-hard madness
To lodge snug in my skull
I would you sent me hordes of horses
Galloping
Crushing
But do not break
The yolk of the moon on me.

A leopard lives in a Muu tree
Watching my home
My lambs are born speckled
My wives tie their skirts tight
And turn away –
Fearing mottled offspring.
They bathe when the moon is high
Soft and fecund
Splash cold mountain stream water on their nipples
Drop their skin skirts and call obscenities.
I'm besieged
I shall have to cut down the muu tree
I'm besieged
I walk about stiff
Stroking my loins
A leopard lives outside my homestead
Watching my women
I have called him elder, the one-from-the-same-womb
He peers at me with slit eyes
His head held high
My sword has rusted in the scabbard.
My wives purse their lips
When owls call for mating
I'm besieged
They fetch cold mountain water
They crush the sugar cane
But refuse to touch my beer horn.
My fences are broken
My medicine bags torn
The hair on my loins is singed
The upright post at the date has fallen

My women are frisky
The leopard arches over my homestead
Eats my lambs
Resuscitating himself.

Greet for me the son of Karanja
Tell him for me I greet him
When the goats are gathered
And dusk trembles
Waiting, waiting
Greet for me Wanyoike
Son of Karanja

Oooi . . . oooi . . . Aaaiya

Tell him I'll come
I'll meet him
Carrying with me
Two twin sticks
Straight as an arrow
And as fast
Will bring with me
Two sapling youths
To kill me the Maitha
Pungent as snuff
Swift

Oooi . . . oooi . . . Aaaiya.

Greet for me the son of Karanja
Tell him to hurry
Or the cows will yield no milk
And his lady refuses to be bled
Greet him tell him to hurry
Or the cobwebs seal his door
A place for broken pots
Where a fire should have been

Oooi . . . oooi . . . Aaaiya.

[66]

The field was full of bruised babies
Blood, hardening
Slowly stealing on ashen faces
Painted open lips.
Women sat reclining
Monuments of peace
Sculptured by death.
The river heaved, eased
Flowed on
The river was gay
Flowing on
For this field was frozen in blood
And the river was leaving.
Boots had trodden this field
Booby traps (set by those
Who had left with the river)
Had gripped babies
In silence.

In the field the dead women
Sighed
Remembering the dull thud
Of the metal fist
Of the interrogator
(These were not the sons of rice)
Remembered
The steely cold of a gun
Placed against the temple
Seeking entrance
No more, no more
Betrayal

The useless pain of snatching
Life from the fertile flood.
In that moment
The women were winnowed
(The dross drifted with the river)
The seed was sown
In blood
Other sons of rice would sprout
Sheathed
For these women
Were sowing
In blood.

The field was rich for
This was not despair
This was fate, pestilence
This silence was not acquiescence
This was patience
This death was eloquent
This was not new
This was the plague of the year before
This would be wiped out.

This was never to be forgotten
For this was not war
As other wars are wars
For chroniclers
These other sons
Had been sent to stir the spirit
(Their blood mingled with the sons of rice)
They would smell this

In the field which
The women
Had sown
In blood.

This seed would spread
Sealed in the marrow
Would spread
In the insane twitch of the mouth
Of those who sailed with the river
Would spread
To the House of Bone
For the river had flowed.

JOSEPH KARIUKI *Blind*

When you left
Without a word,
My heart wept –

Not so much
For lost love
(And a touch),

But the more
For the blinkers
Which I wore

For so long.
For so late
Did I worship
Such an ingrate?

You dragged me
Thorough the gates of pain
To song,
Love from my heart
Spilling over;

Reason, like Lucifer's sin
Burst away and fled.

Now the freer motion
Over the fertile ground
Will reign.

They no longer sleep.
Dissonant machine-gun cracks
And the wails of their dying
Have drowned their dancing drums.
And tomorrow –
Will there be a tomorrow?
They can no longer sleep.

A wind of awakening blowing from the north –
To dispel the despair of life's mockery
So that by death their children may live
Once again as men –
Has called them to resist.

They are not alone:
Their moans find echoes in the torn continent.
And the oppressors shall never again
Till the envied blood-clogged earth
In peace.
They shall no longer sleep.

AMIN KASSAM *Martin Luther King*

Under Abraham's vacant eyes
He proclaimed a dream
A dream
That blossomed a sun
Where darkness had reigned
A dream
That bestrode the eagle
With ringing heart
Wheeling high above
Flailing truncheons thudding
On bare flesh
From rocky desert
He carved a valley
Where soil and clouds
Embraced and fused
With the voice of man
Buried in his neck

AMIN KASSAM *Mombasa*

Village grown large
I return to the womb
Smell of fish and sweat of ages
Stored in a bundle
Of palm leaves
Where bark canoes used to dry
With salt on their spines
Fishermen patching nets
At edge of sea.

Shark spread on table
Under mango tree –
Nearby heaps of cassava
Maize and bananas was market.

Sand and mosquitoes

I remember
A cyclist returned at night
Through empty streets
Still tongue-tied.

warm scent
lingers
to mark his passage
through
leaves and flowers
breathing
perfume
as under
the surveillance of
furtive eyes
he
buries
his mane
of fire
in the darkness
of his paws
and
with
bloodshot eyes
stalks
into the grass.

birds
twitter
with anxiety
at the predator
come
to take
his place
for the night.

Old men wait at the stop
Huddling from rain
Under a tree
As I pass
Running to catch up
With my reflection
In a puddle
They laugh
And talk of death.

YUSUF O. KASSAM *Maji Maji*

Sitting on a stool outside his mud hut,
The mzee scratched his head in a slow motion,
Trying to recall.
His dim grey eyes quiveringly stared into the distance
And with a faint faltering voice he spoke
Of the wind that stirred sinister feelings,
Of the leaves that rustled with foreboding,
Of the men who talked of deliverance and freedom,
And of the warriors who pledged to fight.
Then he paused and snuffed some tobacco
'The Germans –' He shook his head and shuddered:
'Yes, they came – with guns, to be sure –
Many guns.'
His glance slowly shifted in a broken semi-circle
At each of the few listeners who squatted on the ground.
He pointed to the distant hills on his right:
'For many days,
They resounded with drum-beats and frenzied cries;
Then with the spirits of alien ancestors
They thundered with strange unearthly sounds.'
Placing both his hands on his head,
He looked down on the earth and pronounced,
'They fired bullets, not water, no, not water.'
He looked up, with a face crumpled with agony,
And with an unsteady swing of his arm, he said,
'Dead, we all lay dead.'
While the mzee paused, still and silent,
His listeners gravely looked at each other
Seeming to echo his last words in chorus.
Finally, exhausted, he sighed,
'The Germans came and went,
And for many long years
No drums beat again.'

It was that memorable night when I heard it,
Yes, I heard it all.
That night sleep deserted me,
Mocked at me and tantalized me;
So I lay awake, sharp in all my senses.

It was long past midnight:
Time dragged on, the clock wouldn't chime;
The dog wouldn't bark, nor the baby cry;
It was a moonless and windless night;
The whole universe seemed to stagnate
In dark, dreary, dead slumber.
What was amiss? I knew not.

The dead quietness and solitude
Seemed to be eternal, – but
Waves of babbling and muttering
Began to trickle through the street;
A distant roaring of heavy trucks filled the air;
Hurried footsteps echoed through the street.
What was amiss? I knew not.

I pulled my curtain to see,
And there I saw it all –
Heavy boots, thick uniforms and solid helmets,
Dimly discernible under the pale street lamp.
The atmosphere stood stiff and solid with
Brawny-faced and clenched-teeth determination.
Thus the cauldron had boiled that sleepless night.

[78]

The night had pulsed with passions high and wild;
The streets were stained with new portraits framed;
The wheel changed hands and new plans were filed.
The morning saw the country strangely dressed,
And everyone attended the rally
To hear the eloquence from a strange face,
And everyone quietly nodded and said, 'Yes'.

People walk,
But where is the sound of their footsteps?
People talk,
But where is their charm and humour?
It is warm and bright,
But I cannot see the sun!
It is cool and romantic,
But I cannot see the moon!
The trees sway,
Without the rustling of their leaves.
The music plays,
Without rhythm or enchantment.
The lamps light devoid of any glow;
Hot coffee is served devoid of any aroma.
I shake hands but cannot get the grip;
I hit a ball but it does not rise.

Someone pronounces, 'Arise'!
But where is the energy?
Another pleads, 'Enliven'!
But where is the blood?
A third says 'Illuminate'!
But where is the light?

I seek in vain for colour and lustre,
For the dew and spice,
For the warmth and radiance;
Yes, the very soil under my feet lacks fertility.

The drum beats,
And with bare feet and red earth,
Rhythm erupts,
Muscles and drums synchronized.
Bodies sweat,
Vigorously,
Glistening round the flickering fire,
Erotic.
The night is long,
Drums beat more furiously,
Moving the kaleidoscope of frenzied expressions,
And the pulse outruns the drum beat.
The drums inspired the dancers,
Now the dancers inspire the drummers.
No more.
Relax.
Wipe the dust and the sweat.
But the pulse still beats,
Muscles twitch,
And drums echo,
All in a hangover of rhythm,
African rhythm.

YUSUF O. KASSAM *The Recurrent Design*

The sun set, night came, and everything was dark:
It was a signal to stir.
Out in the rough sea the propeller churned,
And the bewildered rudder trailed behind;
The shovel dug the ground mile after mile;
Heavy rubber smouldered on lonely roads;
Chains of steel-plate crushed the plants and the stones,
While a droning echo filled the pierced sky.

Soon the sea, the land, the sky were all quiet;
The sweat was wiped and the pistons rested,
And all the movement came to a standstill.

Then came the long and nervous waiting:
The clock ticked,
The heart beat,
The sentry stepped,
The eyes gleamed,
And the morse peeped under a cold finger.

At dawn the clock pointed the hour, and
'Strike', shrilled the sharp calculated command.
At once the fever and the frenzy mushroomed,
While the rising sun splashed red everywhere:
Those who were then beginning to awake
Never awoke again.

YUSUF O. KASSAM *The Splash*

Under warm sunshine,
A pond of water rests, calm and serene.
The blue sky inhabits the middle of the pond,
And its sides reflect the greenery,
Spotted with the yellow and the red,
The red and the violet.
The water, the sky, the vegetation,
Hand in hand convey harmony and peace.
Then comes the splash!
And a tremendous stirring surges:
Reflections distort,
Giving way to a rushing flow of ripples,
Ripples concentric,
Ripples innumerable,
All fleeing from the wound.
Time elapses,
Ripples fade,
Reflections regain their shape,
And once again emerges the pond
Smooth and tranquil.
But the stone!
The stone will always cling to the bottom.

i confess ive never met a chinese who looks old
but im told hell really look old

antiquity and china are twins
dont confuse confucius with buddha
tho both are sages oriental ancient

i woke this morning
to find lincoln down
and george washington lying
on the ground a statue

surely confucius must live
if only to prolong the rarity

the chairman says no
the gavel rules the day

senghor knows
where the vote comes from

sir
where does culture go

to atoms
the child says

   the gentle idiots who
   cannot scare the crow

we guard the ways of old
and dont forget the church

abhorring shedding blood
successes holy mark

macbeth had done the deed
before he went to sleep

let the old man die
with his hospitality
and humanism

till nile flows back
victoria lake

TABAN LO LIYONG from: *The Marriage of Black and
White*

IV

Marry me
And we shall have children
Who will not need sunbathing
Having been blessed with a skin
The hue that is intermediate:
True representatives
Of the race of the future:
Of the conscience that is to be
A consensus of all there is
Of culture and skins:
People who speak a language
That is universal
As the stocks from which it is derived:
The product of prides in races;
The successors over petty bigotry:
The race that will inherit
The best there is from both;
Children grown strong
Tempered by ill-knowledges
That are appendixes
In the two camps
Of colour curtains.

And Nietzsche was wrong
Against racial mixing;
He is right – if
There is no psychological homework.

My skin is so black
And potent as the coal
That the miners bring out
From the bowels of the earth,
With plenty of energy entrapped.

[86]

Since the world is everyday traversed
By Eskimos and the Deserters alike:
Dwellers of adverse climates
With built-in protections for their own niches.
It is so clear that the issues
Of parents from the extremes
Are more favoured to live stronger
Than the parents blind in one eye.

C'mon
We are not freaks,
We are of the same species
Despite the protective colouration,
Nature's own invention
For her sons' accommodations
To the various latitudes
Before the sons could conquer
Distance.

We are not freaks
I mean you are not and I am not.
And our children won't be mules —
Dead ends of crossbreedings —
On the contrary, very robust,
Best fitted to live in this their world,
A world relative and comparative,
A world shrunk by Orville and Marconi,
A world that knows no boundary,
A world in flux,
With the colour disc in full swing
Blurring the primaries,
A world betterworsened by
I-it.

[87]

Gloria Bishop
Perhaps I yearn to be mothered
And you fitted in very well;
Perhaps you needed children
And we obliged;

I had the chance to sit on your lap
And be patted on the head,
And be told:
Son, your world is yours,
Go and play now,
Come back for suck
Otherwise amuse yourself.

And sometimes:
Let's look at Whitman.
And I told the class:
Whitman said to Prostitute:
C'mon, get off the street,
Go home and wash yourself clean,
For tonight, I Whitman,
Will be your guest.

The class laughed,
I don't know why,
Cheap morality, perhaps.

Gloria,
You don't know a lot
(And that's an asset for successful teaching)

[88]

But you have unbounded energy
And the knack to direct our vision
Over the contours of literature
And these place you above everybody else.

Thanks be to you —
You were my confessor,
My encourager,
My inspiration.

A second mother to me.

XVIII

Nothing makes me madder
Than to find I am not the first
Where I was blazing a trail.

Scarcely six years old
I heard there were machines
Travelling up the air and under water.

I resolved to invent a one
That would fly like a plane
Under earth.

  Certain animals
  Already do that
  I was told.

  Confound them!
Let small pox, great pox, goat pox, pox pox,
pix pox, pax pox, prax prox, prix prix prax,
pix pax pox, pox them!

VI

When I was young mother told me to shut up
  or else the ten-eyed giant would hear me.
When I was young mother told me to finish my food
  or else daddy would spank me dead.
When I was young sister told me to steal
  or else I would not get my meal.
When I was young mother told me to bathe
  or else the *akula* would catch me at night.
When I was young I was told to be home at night
  or else *abiba* would eat my liver.
When I was young teachers told me to pray at night
  or else Satan would be by my side.

Now that I am old the giant comes and visits me:
  I can see his red ten eyes and bloody teeth;
Now that I am old I can feel the hand of father
  when with rage he beats me as if I was a foe;
Now that I am old I still remember sister
  when hunger comes and gnaws my entrails;
Now that I am old I know the Black Maria for sure
  as the truck to take me for cutting up;
Now that I am old I know the eagle overhead is for sure
  that bird which eats my life while I am alive;
Now that I am old I go to pray
  in order to get some quiet.

Never has the death of a poet
Been tolled by all the world,
God's work on earth, though,
Has its universal funeral in the west,
Recurrent grave of day's mighty soul.

Never was a victory so trumpeted,
As that of the sun climbing his fiery way
And then in gorgeous colours falling,
Trailing stars.
Life and death, water and aridity
Bow to his passing ray.

With his passing death stirs in the thicket.
In church the bell is tolled.
In barracks at the last bugle note,
Soldiers like ants file.
The busy woman scolds her child,
Drunkards like sick dogs retch homewards,
The night voice is a harsh guitar.

But on a hill among *musizi* trees
Sweet nuns sing litanies,
Of that virgin whose Son we know.
Priests like lamp-posts in a graveyard,
Stoop over the breviary.
There's a piping of crickets in the bush,
And a bellowing of frogs –
All sing the ancient elegy
For the sun that has died in the West.

STEPHEN LUBEGA *Requiem for Kagumba*

Irreconcilable love and pity
Butted against my heart;
For my gentlest and kindest,
The bravest and humblest friend, Kagumba,
Dipped his life in a river.

Uganda's ring champion
Could not jab the mighty waters of Mayanja;
With his Diploma in Education
Could not teach the river
(Do not laugh, friends)
But with six others
His body submitted to the water.

I entered a gloomed grief
That was handed down to me
While still a child
By my gone grandmother.
I swallowed the best of my smiles
And gave a timid bow to Death.
A hundred fears poured into my shrunken heart
As fast as waves against a wreck.
Gloved grief punched and hooked
My ego
Only to crown me with dark haloes.

JOHN S. MBITI *The Crucified Thief*

I am a crucified thief,
Dying for my unnumbered sins;
Beside me dies the 'sinful' God
Who takes away the sin of the world.

His fingers freeze from cold,
His eyes are dark with desert dust,
His throat is coarse from thirst.
He suffers thus for me and you.

I am a crucified thief,
Stealing away the love of God,
I am crucified with Christ,
To be with Him in paradise.

The sun above for fear hides,
The earth beneath in pain shakes,
And buried souls awake to weep,
While angels bow and wink in tears.

Alone I stole, I stole
But here with Christ I die.
He dies for crucified thieves,
And steals their sins away.

JOHN S. MBITI *New York Skyscrapers*

The weak scattered rays of yellow sun
Peeped through the hazy tissues
That blanketed them with transparent wax.
And as the wrinkled rays closed the day,
Smoky chimneys of New York coughed
Looking down in bended towers,
And vomited sad tears of dark smoke.

As the wrinkled rays dismissed the day
Smoky chimneys of New York coughed
Vomiting chunks of thick smoke
Like rotten rust scraped
From their towering heights.

Dispersed and weak
The shafts of yellow rays
Descend
Peeping through the hazy tissues
That blanket them with transparent wax.

JOHN S. MBITI *My Father's Wooden House*

Let not your grinning ads lure me
But leave me in my father's wooden house
Unseen
Amidst the woods of Africa's sunny plains
Surrounded by apes and hippos
Discerning the jazz of nocturnal birds and bugs.
Let me close to mother earth remain
Embraced in her Nature's rugged cloak.
Out of this my lowly home
Proceed my faithful dog to hunt,
The herdsboy removes to tender sheep and cows,
And evening hours in Nature's mirth abound
Around the smoky wooden fire
Which warms my father's wooden house.

Oh Manhattan Manhattan!
The chiefest isle beyond the seas,
I envy you not,
I covet not your naked thighs
Artificially dyed in Parisian perfumes
And on the beach soliciting summer's tan,
With all your noisy calls to purchase
The latest mechanical gadgets
Whilst I with my slackening muscles work
And toil with Nature
Under my feet and about my way.
Manhattan in all your conglomerate noises
Of muddled trains and trucks and cars and helicopters
Bustling ceaselessly through your calendars,
Running and never resting:
Dull you remain to those tender touches
Of man's friendships and love

Laughing with a gilded row of movable teeth
The symbol of your artificial ways.

So let me abide in Nature's threshold
Cautiously treading on the paths of cobras black,
And sleep on warping wooden beams
Overlain with antelope's hairy leather
Wearing and eating of Nature's overflows:
But let my feeling human heart
Forever remain with me,
Let me spend my years counting
The open stars above my head,
And let me greet my kin and neighbour
With a heart of love.
But you lofty Manhattan
With picture printed cards
Your sons and daughters greet
Par avion across the seas,
And let the sleeping pills
Your health sustain.

Shall I compare your towering majesty
Oh Manhattan,
To our grassy stubble roofs?
Yours is the vast road with cars and cans and banks,
But leave me unmolested
My gravel path to plod,
Holding the shepherd's crooked rod.
Oh leave me in my father's wooden house
Close to Nature,
And close to kin, neighbour and friend.

JOHN S. MBITI *War After War*

We are tired of waiting for another war
Our trees their leaves have shed
The winter has come and gone
Spring flowers have blossomed and withered
And here we are
Still waiting for another war
Our atom bombs have rusty grown
And bald are the heads of those who made them
But we
The ugly martyrs of another war
Do not fear
We have seen wars
We know their taste is sweet
And their smell is good
Smoke from the guns is all we dream about
Waiting for our opulent leaders
To start another war
Waiting
Till the first shot is heard
And the war trumpet is blown

JOHN S. MBITI *Wearing Masks of Fear*

We are the solitary street travellers,
Fearing death
And wearing masks of fear.

We've been waiting here
In the middle of a long narrow street,
Wanting to cross and walk eastward,
Eastward with our backs facing West,
But we fear death . . .
Death before us,
Death from the South and death from the North.

We are the solitary street travellers
Fearing death
And wearing masks of fear.

We are consumed by solitude –
You
    and you
        and I
The three solitary men and women and children,
Fearing death.

We fear to cross the street
And fear to wait in the street
And fear to wear our masks of fear.

Up on a hill it stood immovable,
Dark and gloomy in the dusk;
A heavy silence hung in the air
Restraining her courage, her will;
But on she walked.

A cricket whistled breaking the silence,
Lighting her path and her will;
Then suddenly it stopped,
As if suppressed by a heavy hand,
Still – on she moved.

Every move drew her nearer,
Every move gravitated towards the gloom;
Giant trees, heavy and dark before her rose,
Guards on duty, erect in the dark,
Through them – she pushed.

With eyes closed, arms outstretched,
She groped in an envelope of black;
The air grew dense and doomed,
Her heart drummed faster and louder;
To the door – she stepped.

With trembling hands she pushed,
A squeal pierced the air;
Flashes blinded her sight;
And down she descended at a blow,
On the grim, rude stone.

With dazzling eyes: sweet poison in teeth,
He to the core armed plays his game;
Triumphantly the fools applaud,
While the wise weigh;
With feet on edge, mouth in mid-air
He cunningly his prey surveys;
Then suddenly he aims his shot:
Fool and wise applaud,
The game is won,
In the centre firmly he stands:
Luxuriously flies by that time.

The time has flown: no fruit has yet emerged:
Fool and wise their heads together bend;
Meanwhile he comfortable puffs his pipe,
Belching the while for the richness of it all;
Then suddenly –
Eyes open: ears unstop
As the crowd clamours,
Clamours for its share:
Eyes left – right –
Up and down he stares,
Starts –

Gripping the table he aims his shot:
Once sweet, bitter becomes the poison:
Edgeward blows the storm,
Persists – accelerates
Arms outstretch
Eyes madly dart;
Topples – and stares into darkness.

I'll put aside my hoe:
Let them call me lazy.
I'll lay aside my stick:
Let my cattle rove alone.
I'll bid farewell my girl
And my laughing sister
Despite their sweet tears.
I'll pat my younger brother.
Then I'll go and kneel down
Before the two heaps of stones
Where my parents lie;
I'll plead with them to call
The blessing of their gods
On me, a troubled youth,
Before I go in the pursuit.

Then I'll gird my loin-cloth.
Sling my bow and the sword
Of my clan. Spear in hand
I'll go to face the foe.
The dewy grass shall be
My couch; on the cold rock
My head shall rest;
The damp night air shall blanket me;
And to the wild beast
I'll be a guest.
I'll drink from the wandering streams;
Suck on wild fruits.
Till I have faced my foe
I'll be ashamed to face my home.
Courage, hate and my enemy's fate
Drive me on. Mighty he stands

But curse be on me if
I show him my naked heels:
No! Never, never!
Come death before surrender
But I'll slay him – this I know.

Then I'll dry my bleeding
Sword on my thirsty tongue;
And proclaim victory –
The will of my fathers.
Thus, all having been done,
And my poor heart settled,
I'll venture to go home.
I'll take up my hoe and dig;
I'll pick up my stick and herd;
I'll court my girl and wed.
Having done my duty,
I'll sit by the fire
And grow old.

PAUL MUKASA-SSALI *Katebo Port*

There's a strong wind that breaks on Katebo Port,
Murmuring and throbbing like a dim, dirge drum,
And, welling roaring waves like a full-throated song,
Knocks at one's inner spirit with its swagger.
It's there we went fishing on memorable afternoons
The pebbled beach stretched out wet and gleaming
With granite cliffs rising crescent in translucent light:
Livid and layered, pocked with tiny caves.
The canoes painted in gaudy greens, blues and reds
With the soft smack of the water lapping their flanks
Suggesting the colourful gaiety of canoe regattas
The fishermen squatted, mending their nets,
Agile young men with untidy beards.
The women with slung, crying babies on their backs
Came in groups to buy sweet, slit smoked fish.
Evening came and people went away
Except for the watchful boys with catapults ready
To shoot at the low-flying birds from the lake.

PAUL MUKASA-SSALI *The Sentinel*

The rising sun on a Sunday morning
Sometimes catches the night sentinel
Unawares,
Curled in his sleep like an apostrophe,
Still dotty with a drowsy mouth –
Obnoxiously open
As if starting a tentative yawn.

When you come, dear friend,
Don't surprise me at the blink of dawn
With your dew-wet shuffling of footsteps
On the stair and along the corridor.
When you come, dear friend,
Give me word, drop me a line
But don't surprise me in bed unshaven
Smelling of sleep with no pyjama coat!
Besides, my room at that apprehensive hour
With sprawled clothes and towel on the chair
Would be unforgettably chaotic.
But when you come, dear friend,
Don't be exasperating and keep me waiting
So that I pace about the room – alone,
Or put a disc on the record-player,
Waiting for your any-minute knock on the door.

There she lay in a pool of blood,
Speared and maimed,
Mute and lifeless,
Base and worthless.

There she lay, the butchered woman,
The butchered woman, daughter of a chief,
The daughter of a chief, the town beauty,
Silenced by the rage of a spear.

She lay in a pool of blood, nude as she was born,
Fierce, as if hours ago not lovely to touch,
Already beginning to steam like fresh dung:
No one knew she was daughter of a chief.

She lay mid a group of frightened women –
Women who were mad with grief.
Men that were there fumed with fury
That a beauty should enter the ground so young.

There she lay, silenced for ever,
With her beauty crossed,
Her eyes for ever shut to the world;
Soon the ground was to swallow her.

Oo, from which wing do you come?
Darling, I am all done:
It's the blood in my veins that speaks to you!
Darling, just days ago – just days ago
I was married in the church to a tin of salt.
If only I was powerful – if only I was powerful,
The church would cut us asunder,
Then I'd marry you:
I'd sacrifice all to bring us together.
Darling, feel my unlucky body
And see how much I've cooled –
Cooled because I – I don't know
Whether you can admit a second-hand wife –
A second-hand wife to your bed.
Whatever you ask me, your old girl-friend,
I will obey.
After the marriage he left me a widow,
Left me husbandless, so young a girl,
And he went to a college in the States.
Am I his sister? Very no!
And, to be sure, I can't sexually starve:
I hope with you he'll find me gone;
With you I'll be gone if you agree.
Dear, that's all I have to say;
But without you, for sure, I'll die unhappy.

Path-let . . . leaving home, leading out,
Return my mother to me.
The sun is sinking and darkness coming,
Hens and cocks are already inside and babies drowsing,
Return my mother to me.
We do not have fire-wood and I have not seen the lantern,
There is no more food and the water has run out,
Path-let I pray you, return my mother to me.
Path of the hillocks, path of the small stones,
Path of slipperiness, path of the mud,
Return my mother to me.
Path of the papyrus, path of the rivers,
Path of the small forests, path of the reeds,
Return my mother to me.
Path that winds, path of the short-cut,
Over-trodden path, newly-made path,
Return my mother to me.
Path, I implore you, return my mother to me.
Path of the crossways, path that branches off,
Path of the stinging shrubs, path of the bridge,
Return my mother to me.
Path of the open, path of the valley,
Path of the steep climb, path of the downward slope,
Return my mother to me.
Children are drowsing about to sleep,
Darkness is coming and there is no fire-wood,
And I have not found the lantern:
Return my mother to me.

The kraal fence
    hides quarrels
Of jealous wives,
    it hides the miseries within
and sadness
    of wives fallen from favour.
It excludes anyone
    beyond its gate
That reed fence
    spells laughter, joy
and happiness to the outside
    but hides the cruelty
of the husband within
    to the tortured tormented wife,
the sad one full of woes:
    the favoured one full of ease and joy.
Yes, that reed fence hides plenty.

Alone in the vast forest of elders
A young tree grows
Dreaming of days she'll be accepted
Surrounded by her silent mates
And beardy elders
She is gay and sad and happy, yet
Not knowing why.

Among the majesty of beardy elders
Wrapped in tottering beauty
Tinged with grey
Knowing for once and all
She never will be happy with her lot
Till her branches touch the blue

Alone with her silent mates
Alone among beardy elders
Her mind meanders across
Broody shadows of time growing old,
Time arrested at dawn
Reaching out for peace
Amidst the elders of time.

A limping little cupid of farce
An allegory of mortality.
Neither smile nor tears are
Capable of ushering in this uncertainty,
The Darling of Fate.
She knows his time is winged.
Papyrus-reeds dewy shaken
In a misty-grey morning
Splattering with rain drops and
The hooting Owl.
Head free of hair, and papyrus-reeds
Wound like a witch's snake
Around her neck,
        Makoha!
A collection of dung-heap
Inevitable earth, an
Ash Wednesday.

When you have whispered it in my cocked ear
With an equivocal voice and quivering frame;
When you have sworn it was by me
And not Tom, Dick, or Harry;
When you have recreated the memorable scene
That night after the Charity Ball
When the heroine of contrived action
Clutched at the elusive moment of emaciated hope;
When you have concluded with a certain smile
That the D.C. would do it secretly –
Modena, do not mock the bruised bosom of the widowed
   mother
When I make discoveries and speak truths
Which we both knew but never revealed:
How you explained your week-end absences
By attending imaginary funerals of imaginary relatives;
How you realized your battered frame,
Like stale beer that has lost its spear,
Would not find any other male patron;
How you gave me hurried promotions
From boy-friend to lover and then to fiancé;
How you baited me with your selfish generosity;
Do not mock the wounded heart of the widowed mother
When I promise you that I'll not keep an oath
Extorted from me by your forked tongue;
Do not fool mankind any more
With elegies of innocence, chastity and youth;
Let the sun melt all the rings on men's fingers –
After the first treachery, there is no other.

RICHARD NTIRU *The Pauper*

Pauper, pauper, craning your eyes
In all directions, in no direction!
What brutal force, malignant element,
Dared to forge your piteous fate?
Was it worth the effort, the time?

You limply lean on a leafless tree
Nursing the jiggers that shrivel your bottom
Like a baby newly born to an old woman.
What crime, what treason did you commit
That you are thus condemned to human indifference?

And when you trudge on the horny pads,
Gullied like the soles of modern shoes,
Pads that even jiggers cannot conquer:
Does He admire your sense of endurance
Or turn his head away from your impudent presence?

You sit alone on hairless goatskins,
Your ribs and bones reflecting the light
That beautiful cars reflect on you,
Squashing lice between your nails
And cleaning your nails with dry saliva.

And when He looks at the grimy coating
Caking off your emaciated skin,
At the rust that uproots all your teeth
Like a pick on a stony piece of land,
Does He pat his paunch at the wonderful sight?

Pauper, pauper, crouching in beautiful verandas
Of beautiful cities and beautiful people,
Tourists and I will take your snapshots,
And your M.P. with a shining head and triple chin
Will mourn your fate in a supplementary question at
  Question Time.

Only those
Who have survived
The final anaesthetization;
Those who have enacted the final epilogue;
Only these
Have the prescient perception
Of the inner idea of life
And can partake of the spectral dance;

Only they
Have the inner knowledge
Of the numbing nutation
On gravestill nights when nude priests,
In mortal ecstasy,
Bless multicoloured antiamulets
On virgin pelvicbone amphorae
And celebrate prenatal deathdays
To the rhythm of the drum of death
Struck with the thighbone
Of him who died on his bridal night.

These are they
Who have bared their bones
And submitted to the savage salvation
Of the caustic dew of the cold grave;
Only these
Understand the eloquence of the silence
Between two echoes in a haunted cave.

Who but they
Who walk beyond the twilight glimmer
Between sleep and waking,

Who bask in nocturnal sunlight
And breathe the cool diurnal darkbreeze,
Who have experienced
The realization of the inevitable dream,
Know the revitalizing power of the stilled blood?

But we,
We who clutch at tattered totems
And turn away from solar solace
When the innocence butter
Melts in our hands at the ordeal,
We who raise open hands in supplication to Nyabingi –
Hands that would embrace –
What dream are we capable of?

RICHARD NTIRU *Virgine Madre*

Virgine Madre
daughter of her son
mother of her son
Musaba's marriage
was not meant to last
divorce due to incompatibility
perhaps there were antecedents
she had a premarital son
George defied abortion
Virgine Madre
Baine could get himself a new wife
Musaba a new husband
or characters to that effect

music by the cranes
the cranes on the stage

Musaba must not miss her new lover
hair imported from Northern Canada
intense products of I.C.I.
islands of nature amid a sea of civilization
shades of black on a background of sickly yellow
self-suffocation
in cheap resplendent dress
as taut as her soul
betraying a large floppy behind
supported on two rickety thighs
(alas the stockings hung loose)
tapering to shoes three inches off the ground
she sat in the humid ballroom
issuing incense
from her I.C.I. manufactory

[118]

George belched in her face
and haggled for a dance
the price was a bottle of waragi
swig
and it was gone
she staggered on the floor awhile
she was led by the back door . . .
the lights winked for five minutes
they were shy to see the sight

O leka nnyabo togenda

she transcended advice
the price was one pound
for incest . . .

I hear sweet voice and my heart beats.
Who calls? Does someone call outside?
Bellowing winds? Wind drowns all.
From bedside pillow
I hear voices of leaves
Quiver in wind blown by zephyr
Hear rivers speak and springs whisper;
Birds whistle, insects click by.
Do you hear voices of leaves?
    I hear someone call
    My heart beats
    And drums, throbs like water-pump.

Voices from the dark
From forest deep
    Whistling leaves
Who calls?
I hear voices from wind talking
Sound that shuttles me
Between
Echo and ears.
I hear trees talking
See them wiping tears
Their feet trickle with gore.

Don't you see trees walking
Trample in frenzy, dance
And climb my veins
Talking then recede like sail-away
Oar-boats on and on away
Where sky lips kiss
Distant hills and sea

Where sun abdicates from sky
In silence
Sound of brave paddles die
Like stalks of men not
Good for firewood lying
Deserted like school in holiday
Overgrown with loneliness

Nothing breaks the silence of sleep's territory,
Only you and me,
Tree and Star,
Knees rubbing,
Cheeks melting and cooling
In the sag and thrust of billowing;
Loving
With the power of wilderness
And the constance of Life,
Growing and deepening with each new sun
And every new moon.
You and me
Us
We
Together in the eternity of passion.
We came together in the quiet heat
Of tropical night;
I ask not from whence passion comes
But accept the challenge of your boiling breasts.
Tropical night in December
Night of passionate abandon,
Cool glittering stars fused and fusing
In the blackness of never ending sky;
But all too soon
The whip of Crosses
Will rip the bliss of our
Lango night in December
And save your breasts for the Omnipotent
Bites of the teeth of worms!

OKELLO OCULI *The Return*

Dawn is breaking
Behind the hut and a vague glow marching
Out, boldly,
A herald!
Like hot breaths of grass fire,
Bewitching bouncing frantic grasshoppers
And the sly glide of the chameleon.
There is a dim stirring in the bushes;
A Gasp as of a child in battle with
Waking.
A forlorn squeal of a tiny bird
Awakes the rest!
Their beaks grope the stubborn but
Yielding clouds of Darkness,
Rising in longing,
Surging in growing chorus of impatient,
Frantic and dizzy beaks rushing to Dawn
The rush to dawn
To solve the riddle that lies deeply
In the wrinkled faces
And troubled eyes of the Natives.

I go to my old father
He is sitting in the shade at the foot of the simsim granary,
His eyes are fixed on the three graves of his grandchildren
He is silent.

Father, I say to him,
Father, gather the bridewealth so that I may marry the
    girl of my bosom!

My old father rests his bony chin in the broken cups of his
    withered hands,
His long black finger-nails vainly digging into the tough
    dry skin of his cheeks
He keeps staring at the graves of his grandchildren,
Some labikka weeds and obiya grasses are growing on the
    mounds.
My old father does not answer me, only two large clotting
    tears crawl down his wrinkled cheeks,
And a faint half smile alights on his lips, causing them to
    quiver and part slightly.

He reaches out for his walking staff, oily with age and
    smooth like the long teeth of an old elephant.
One hand on his broken hip, he heaves himself up on the
    three stilts,
His every joint crackling and the bones breaking!
Hm! he sighs, and staggers towards the graves of his
    grandchildren,
And with the bony-dry staff he strikes the mounds: One!
    Two! Three!
He bends to pluck the labikka weeds and the obiya grasses,

[124]

But he cannot reach the ground, his stone-stiff back cracks
   like dry firewood.
Hm! he sighs again, he turns around and walks past me.
He does not speak to me.
There are more clotting tears on his glassy eyes,
The faint smile on his broken lips has grown bigger.

II

My old mother is returning from the well
The water-pot sits on the pad on her grey wet head.
One hand fondles the belly of the water pot, the other
   strangles the walking staff.
She pauses briefly by the graves of her grandchildren and
   studies the labikka weeds and the obiya grasses waving
   like feathers atop the mounds.

Hm! she sighs
She walks past me;
She does not greet me.
Her face is wet, perhaps with sweat, perhaps with water
   from the water-pot
Perhaps some tears mingle with the water and sweat
The thing on her face is not a smile,
Her lips are tightly locked.

She stops before the door of her hut
She throws down the wet walking staff, klenky, klenky!
A little girl in green frock runs to her assistance;
Slowly, slowly, steadily she kneels down;
Together, slowly, slowly, gently they lift the water-pot and
   put it down.
My old mother says, Thank you!

Some water splashes onto the earth, and wets the little
    girl's school books.
She bursts into tears, and rolls on the earth, soiling her
    beautiful green frock,
A little boy giggles.
He says, All women are the same aren't they?
Another little boy consoles his sister.

III

I go to the Town
I see a man and a woman
He wears heavy boots, his buttocks are like sacks of cotton
His chest resembles the simsim granary,
His head is hidden under a broad-rimmed hat.

In one hand he holds a loaded machine-gun, his fingers at
    the trigger
His other hand coils round the waist of the woman like a
    starving python.
They part after a noisy kiss
Hm! he sighs!
Hm! she sighs!

He marches past me, stumping the earth in anger, like an
    elephant with a bullet in his bony head!
He does not look at me
He does not touch me, only the butt of his weapon
    touches my knee lightly,
He walks away, the sacks of cotton on his behind rising and
    falling alternately,

Like a bull hippo returning to the river after grazing in
    the fresh grasses.
Hm! I sigh!

I go to the woman,
She does not look up to me,
She writes things in the sand.
She says, How are my children?
I say, Three are dead, and some labikka weeds and obiya
    grasses grow on their graves.
She is silent!
I say, your daughter is now in Primary Six, and your little
    boys ask after you!

The woman says, My mother is dead!
I am silent!
The agoga bird flies overhead
He cries his sorrowful message:
    She is dead! She is dead!
The guinea-fowl croaks in the tree near by
    Sorrow is part of me,
    Sorrow is part of me. How can I escape
    The boldness on my head?
She is silent!
Hm! I sigh!
She says, I want to see my children!

I tell the woman I cannot trace her father.
I say to her I want back the bridewealth that my father
    paid when we wedded some years ago,
When she was full of charm, a sweet innocent
    little hospital ward-maid.

[127]

She is silent!
I tell the woman I will marry the girl of my bosom
I tell her the orphans she left behind will be mothered, and
    the labikka weeds and obiya grasses
        that grow on the graves of her children
        will be weeded,
And the ground around the mounds will be kept tidy.
Hm! she sighs!
She is silent!
I am silent!

The woman reaches out for her handbag.
It is not the one I gave her as a gift last Christmas.
She opens it,
She takes out a new purse,
She takes out a cheque.

She looks up to me, our eyes meet again after many
    months.
There are two deep valleys on her cheeks that were not
    there before
There is some water in the valleys.
The skin on her neck is rotting away,
They say the doctor has cut open her stomach and
    removed the bag of her eggs
So that she may remain a young woman for ever.

I am silent!
A broad witch-smile darkens her wet face,

She screams,
Here, take it! Go and marry your bloody woman!
I open the cheque
It reads,
Shillings One thousand four hundred only!

OKOT P'BITEK *They Sowed and Watered*

They sowed and watered
Acres of cynicisms
Planted forests of laughters
Bitter laughters that flowed in torrents
And men shed tears as they rocked
And held their chests
And laughed and laughed
The floods of tears turned red

They manured the land
And frustrations sprouted
Bursting the soil
Like young bananas
Fat frustrations flourished fast
Yielding fruits green as gall

On the hillsides
They planted angers
And their blossoms crimson red
Covered the hills like
February fires
Their prickly leaves hard and yellow
Pricked men's skins
And wounds festered

In the valley
A streamlet trickled
Its waters sluggish thick
Beside the streamlet rotting smelly
A lamb named Freedom
Dead as stone

[130]

A small herds-boy sat on the bank
He threw small stones
Which hit the carcass
Flies rose like white ants
The boy sobbed eyes full of pepper
Ten men stood on the other side
They roared lion-like
And laughed with mirth
The peals of laughter
Poisoned arrows
Hit the boy like swords of steel
And blood from his heart
Anointing the land

A cockerel crows
as a broken axe
Falls at your feet.
Disarmed by time
You stand unashamed,
Crying 'It is not fair'.
Tied by your own hate-traps
And fouled by the urine
of your flag-bearers,
You have gambled away
the labours of our motherland;
entered trade with death
to batter humanity
with the wave of a flywhisk.
You have locked up the fires
Of living youth,
Damned in the torrents
of conscience
and drenched your entrails
with greed and with pride.

But you have lost the bet
and your line shall we
ostracise
Bury the stool of your mother's house
for vengeance is unleashed
and contempt is in our spittle.
And as public office
Zigzags corrupt
like the trail of a drunken whore
that menstruates,

and as gunmen freely execute
insane commands
We know that the time
has come to kill,
To cleanse,
To free our motherland
From the grip of a gambler.

Atieno washes dishes,
Atieno plucks the chicken,
Atieno gets up early,
Beds her sacks down in the kitchen,
Atieno eight years old,
Atieno yo.

Since she is my sister's child
Atieno needs no pay,
While she works my wife can sit
Sewing every sunny day:
With her earnings I support
Atieno yo.

Atieno's sly and jealous,
Bad example to the kids
Since she minds them, like a schoolgirl
Wants their dresses, shoes and beads,
Atieno ten years old,
Atieno yo.

Now my wife has gone to study
Atieno is less free.
Don't I keep her, school my own ones,
Pay the party, union fee,
All for progress: aren't you grateful
Atieno yo?

Visitors need much attention,
All the more when I work night.
That girl spends too long at market,
Who will teach her what is right?
Atieno rising fourteen,
Atieno yo.

Atieno's had a baby
So we know that she is bad.
Fifty fifty it may live
And repeat the life she had
Ending in post-partum bleeding,
Atieno yo.

Atieno's soon replaced.
Meat and sugar more than all
She ate in such a narrow life
Were lavished on her funeral.
Atieno's gone to glory,
Atieno yo.

I see a road
that runs a hole through a heart
and little cars travelling fast
to further a dream
of little will o' the wisp
holding a spectre of a flower
and blowing kisses in the wind,

that floats a soothing voice
a cry to a heart new-filled to the brim
and love and longing stir it to ripeness
affection lifts the soul
and dizzies the body to grope in a vacuum
For that which is gone
on that road to Mombasa
and little will o' the wisp
holds a spectre of a flower
and blows kisses in the wind.

The moon's lustre opens a yellow flower
looking through blue eyes
flashing diamonds
a spark explodes in a grabbing heart
as it plucks out this flower
to treasure in a box at a corner
of a near-broken house
love beckons little will o' the wisp
as three hundred miles slice a heart in two
leaving a part in me
and flying the other half
three hundred miles.

DAVID RUBADIRI *Death at Mulago*

Towers of strength
granite
hard concrete
enduring
like life itself.

Up they rise
tall and slender
and around them
white coats flit
like the magic they spell.

New Mulago Hospital
– the name shakes—
she stood firmly
on that cool afternoon
giving names, tribe and sex,
A woman clad in busuti.

As the fullstop was entered
on a white sheet of paper
a whitecoat gave a nod.

Her hands cross her chest
and the message unsaid
crushing granite and concrete
in gushing tears of pain
and a lonely sorrow.

DAVID RUBADIRI *Paraa Lodge – to J. H. S.*

I have walked
in the still dark hours of day
and seen elephants graze
and hippos snuggle
shitting in the Nile;
An American party
noisy and childishicited
shitting in cisterns
at Paraa Lodge –
Animal seeing Animal
each asking questions,
and nature
rolling around
like sea-sick billows
to the shore
in the darkness of space,
and us
standing on tidal waves
of engulfing life
embracing
not for comfort –
watched and prayed
for an answer.

DAVID RUBADIRI *The Prostitute*

I desired her
truly, like all men
in the dark cascades
of the Suzana desire beautiful
and seductive women;
the Congo beat
rippled through her
shimmering
along a bottom
down to her feet.

The morning of the night
burst through my thighs
in a longing of fire –
She
almost a goddess
Lit
in clever cascades
of light.
But in the light of another morning,
after the jingle of pennies
how could I move
to stir the glue-pot?

Major Christopher Okigbo was shot dead in Biafra.
Yatuta Chisiza was shot dead in Malawi.
Died that Africa may live with integrity.

CHRISTOPHER OKIGBO

HEAVENSGATE
And LIMITS
Who can reach them?
Lead and barrels of heat
Do so easily.
Youth and love
Joy and faith
Have gone through them,
And now our Limits
Because the lights at Heavens Gate
Have departed

YATUTA CHISIZA

'Old soldiers never die'
The saying goes –
So too to Yatuta
So too to the cause
He lived for.

For us
The rank and file
Only the agony
And the pity
For a piece of lead.

There is much to remember
and little to forget
When greatness
Dies a simple death
For souls of men.

The Witch Tree
old and knobbly
stood with years
scratched by a cross
– abused
as cameras clicked
and learned tongues
– discoursed.

Naked it stood
in its age of mysteries;

Beauty and innocence
stood there too
side by side;
two witches
as I saw them
prismatic lenses prying
the old and the new;
to me she was then
the Mubende Witch Tree.

JOHN RUGANDA *Barricades of Paper Houses*

At dusk, mother
Village crickets chirp
The bruised fortunes
Of the wrinkled
At dawn
The dew will glitter
Yet another hope
For those born
By mothers of tatters.

At dusk, wrinkled one
Slum noses twitch
At tiny anthills
Of faeces
Of the children of kwashiakor
And our scorched throats itch
When dogs with deflated tummies
Hurry to lick shrivelled buttocks
Of the children of kwashiakor.

Yet the tax-man
Will come, as usual
Will come with his chain
And hand-cuffs
And police officers;
Our doglets will bark at them
Will bark at their clean clothes
And their indifference
And we'll go on dodging
Dodging the hand-cuffs
And the police officers
And pailfuls of human dung

In cold prison cells
We'll go on dodging
And leaping
From dust-bins to paper houses
Dilapidated.

What cause have they
These guardians of indifferent laws
What cause have they,
To leave us alone
With our paper houses
And doglets and babylets?

I now hear the rude clang
Of the town clock tower
I hear it scattering the twilight
Behind barricades of paper huts
The rude clang
Scorns my uncertainty
And strips my desolation.
While the shroud of darkness
Lasted
There're no eyes to see
No eyes to see
Decrepit humans
Who're afraid
To look at themselves
In the light and the mirror.

But now the new day
Will bring those who've auctioned

Their tongues
To buy kinship
Of the disciplines of money
Will bring those who've mortgaged
Their honesty
To buy a right
To lurk in the shadows
Of prisoners of power.

They'll soon file past me
To thumb through files
And morning papers
They'll file past me
Putting on party faces
And party shirts
Counting their shuffles indifferently
And I'll go on huddled here
Behind barricades of dust-bins
Till the guardians of hand-cuffs
And pailfuls of human dung
Consume themselves in liquor
I'll go on feeding
On the communal stench
Around this place
The place that's unmindful
Of beatings of a soul
Beaten.

It is the sweet death
Of the God who dies
In Man's birth,
That is the spring of Kato's freedom,
Alike in vanity and divinity;
And it is the victory
Of the God who is
When man dies
That impels Kato,
Not to want heaven,
But the eternal form of pleasure:
For God is
Because man lives.

In the pulpit he swayed and turned.
Leant forward, backward,
To the right: to the left.
His solemn voice echoed;
Lowly the congregation followed,
'Do you love your neighbour?'
Meekly they bow at his keen eye
Now examining a grey head
Heaving under her sobs.
His heart leapt assured –
'Her sins weigh on her!'
So with her he chats outside;
'Weep not child you are pardoned.'
'But, sir, your beard conjured up
The spirit of my dear goat!'

Now when into the far past I pry
With a sharp but puzzled mind
I remember vaguely:
A young girl among towering maize;
Her short uncertain fingers
Pressing one: another
And then another . . .
But where was this field so large?

I remember a large large building
Youngsters resounding,
Twinkles, giggles and tears:
Lost playmates
Now wavering like a dying flame.
Will I ever retrace?
Still far in the past
Faded images will linger.

I remember calm evenings:
A band tamed and captured
By rumbling wonders
Of mighty elephant, witty hare,
Dashing lads and pretty maids.
These readily return:
Not the faces and the voices
Creeping farther and farther.

There she was on the Nile, puffing
The old granny
She puffed
And watched the spirals of smoke
Disappear into the full ethereal emptiness
Counted pebbles as she puffed
Nalangajja, nabalabala, nadding'ana
Arranged them in numerous circles
The honey of the fish flowed
It flowed indifferently, granny or no granny
Then she spat and pondered
Puzzled
Where does the honey come from?
Where does the honey go?
The white egrets drank and bathed
The fish played their innocent games
As the honey of the fish flowed
It flowed indifferently, egrets or no egrets
She threw a pebble into the Nile
And dipped her foot into the Nile
To disturb and provoke its calmness
Ripples formed then disappeared
As the honey of the fish flowed
It flowed indifferently, granny or no granny.

Is this the junction he meant?
Did he say a T-junction or a cross-junction?
Did he mention any traffic lights?
Is that the grocery he mentioned?
Wait a minute, did he say grocery or glossary?
Do you remember?
Did he say a tall building or a bungalow?
Is that the red car he spoke about, which parks there
    always, carrying no soul?
And why is that bus empty?
I wonder how many souls it is capable of carrying . . .
Who is that man going to the petrol station?
Doesn't he know there's no petrol there?
All those empty tanks glaring at him, don't they scare
    him? . . .
Did he say there was a zebra crossing?
Can I cross here?
But where will that lane lead me?
Shall I wait? . . . For what?
Is that the cage he mentioned?
What is in there?
Is it a parrot or a dove?
Yes I remember . . . do I really?
Wait a minute, did he say there are more parrots than
    doves in the world?
Did he really say that, **did** he?
Why should there be more parrots? . . .
Is that the hill he mentioned?
Did he say there was a shrine on the top?
But isn't that a gigantic thorn?
How can I go up there?
What is the thorn doing there?

[150]

Who is it waiting for?
Me? . . .
Suppose I sit here and rest for a few minutes?
Is this broken glass?
Can I sit on these pieces?
Where is the broom?
How can I clean this place?

Unthinking of kids she could be carrying,
I stabbed the cockroach under my heels.
Then I stabbed it again,
A tiny beast –
Stabbed microscopic network of nerves
Until, crushed, belly upwards it lay,
Yellow fluids oozing outwards,
Perhaps ova, perhaps sperm,
Perhaps fluids that sustained life,
Propelling six legs
To detestful destiny now dead.

Grim, with a tense load of murder over me
Yet gloating still in my manhood,
I swept it out of sight;
Unthinking of kids she could be carrying,
For nobody ever thinks of fertility
That gunpowder and napalm
Blows out of a female.

And so, sprinkling water over hands,
Instead of heels that were dirty,
I thought of guilt –
That blunt-edged sword
That is tired of biting conscience.

And I thought I'd write a poem
About death, etc., etc.,
The long lost goodness of man
And the weeping blisters of war.

Then as I sipped in water from the tap,
Unthinking still of kids she might be carrying,
I thought only of war slapping afresh
Unformed flesh hiding in a woman's womb.

Frisk me out, dear,
stand me on border lands of death,
jeer me there,
taunt me, cruel eyes,
freeze blood in my veins,
indifference lurking,
in the greenness of those studs
that hang so gleefully
in the hollow of your eyes.

Forget,
with the inevitable shudder
that speeds down the spine,
that ever I wished to intrude
into tall hedge you built around your beauty.

Forget also,
hard edges of my masculine touch
that crept into softnesses you offered.

Slowly,
as age shall sprinkle
on your face a handful of wrinkles,
shed a few tears of sorrow
over mistakes of youthful years,
as each morrow you shall hear,
from across banished hills
echo of my frenzied laughter.

For I, too, shall have forgiven myself
for madness the likeness of you
must breed in me,

[154]

and know that you too
were a bed-time attraction . . .

no roots, no leaves, no buds
shall blossom between us.

I

the past has boiled itself over
and we are the steam that must flee . . .

i shall summon you therefore,
ancestral spirits of my race,
on this great issue of citizenship,
and you must plead before the minister
for being born so brown.

smile away the hurt of their unfriendly frown
for the sweat is dry
that built the railways,
and black blood must forget
swamp sleeping savagery of greenness
that burst into an indian bazaar,
because the time and tide
and the valour of your business mind
condemned the brown jew
to comb his days in commerce and trade.

black blood of freedom
will soon break your bent shadow,
for you were the criminals of commerce
that daily sucked their coins across the counter.

now they shall look back in anger
the mercedes-benz politicians,
black suited, whisky voiced, swiss bank accounted,
searching in vain
for brown liberals behind the counter
and taunt us about commitment

[156]

for the blood is dry
that roused green savagery
from the slumber of the swamps.

and you will see it always
in back alleys and government offices,
my subordinate asian smile of friendship
that proclaims the jew also is a citizen
and the stare of past hostility replying:
citizen? . . . perhaps so,
but of asian extraction!

i must condemn you therefore,
ancestral spirits of my race,
for wrongful extraction too.

II

but my eyes shall burn again,
a resurrection of brown pride
for i see you now, my father,
fling the victoria cross
into dung-heap of the british empire.

not for your valour
was this false honour on your chest,
but for blood discarded
and bodies dismembered
in white wars of yesterday.
why, then, must i,
your latter-day blood,
bow to live content
with vouchers and quotas?

III

farewell my dear beloved illusions,
for i, too, would have liked to think
only the toes of Africa were infected
but the cancer of colour
has gathered fresh victims now.

black surgeons, too, have prescribed new drugs
and we,
malignant cells,
must fade away soon.

let me not see you now,
ancestral spirits of my race,
in the posture of lawino
lamenting sweetness that has turned sour,
for it shall be my western mind alone
that must summon up an excuse
for the brownness of our sins.

and soon we shall be flying,
unwelcome vultures all over the world,
only to unsheathe fresh wrath
each time we land.

we are the green leaves
that must sprout no more,
for the roots have thrived
on black silence
and false kindness of the white race.

[158]

waste no ceremony
for the unintentionally corrupted;
lead the ram to altar
and wash away the sins of history.

JAGJIT SINGH *Public Butchery*

Some people fear death,
others must face it before a crowd
specially invited
to witness the ceremony of their last breath.

Coups have succeeded elsewhere,
and heads have rolled,
and blood has flown
quite indiscriminately.

But oh! condemned conspirators,
your fate is martyred while you watch,
heads and hearts held high,
dead defiance lurking still
in eyeballs bathed in sweat,

as the judge performs the abortion

for your baby hatched in haste,
before the mother was fully pregnant.

Once you were greeted
and treated
as V I Ps.
now there is blank silence
as a crowd watches
four hooded ministers
hanging in the air.

JOHN SSEMUWANGA *The Blind*

What formless forms do you sense
As you grope after gifts beyond your reach;
What dark beauties do you stare at
As you smile the smile of caged captives;
What longing thoughts lie behind those diseased sockets
As you brood over what might have been;
What sigh do you sigh as we, the fortunate,
Rush past you in search of sun-lit beauties;
What struggle do you stage
As you try to tear apart the blinding shroud;
What pill do you swallow
As you try to live the life of the eyed ones;
What thanks do you give to the Maker who gave us light
And cast you into a dark dark world?

Somewhere in the distance church bells are chiming,
Chiming and beckoning me to the abode of sacred
  mysteries,
Mysteries reverently guarded by cold holy walls;
And my servile soul harks to the angelic melody
And murmurs the words of the third commandment.

It is Sunday morning – and the bells seem to toll
The ebb of ancestral piety,
Piety dimmed by christian chime
And tarnished by rituals ministered by infallible arrivals,
Yet defying latinized devotion
And yearning to woo wayward generations back to time's
  old rituals.

Thus my confused self floats between the two temples
And reveres the God of gods
And communes with the god of yore.

I pose before the candled God
And scent the blessing of the blessed incense
And listen to the words of holy stories,
Stories read from sacred scribes;
And surfeited with heavenly faith I swoon
And crumble down in prostrate adoration.

Yet my sceptical self stealthily wanders
And sits with recusant worshippers
And sings songs of awe
And throbs to the rhythm of reverend music
And bathes in the blood of the white goat
And seems to sigh:
Oh gods, gods, we are lost.

And in dual piety I cry out to God
To water the plains
And the gods whisper:
It will rain.

A stranger's smile captures my untutored heart,
I return the smile with an assuring wink
And tighten the ravelling knot;
Victory pounces on Defeat and eats up a victim,
Victim long trapped in the mystic grip of seeming men.

A painful spasm runs down my spine
And I groan like a sceptic seeing truth:
I, too, have been webbed into the false confidence of
    strange mortals,
Mortals decked in the baffling apparel of stage actors.

We are a strange breed!
Live robots blind to the myriad blends of blood-kins;
Innumerable sons under the self-same roof resembling
    step-fathers;
Cultured numbers living in a world of confused values;
Insane sages devaluating treasures we cherish.

Light is night and darkness day,
Secrecy oozes out on market days,
Truth disintegrates like bubbles on a seasonal pond,
Love dissolves into coined value and betrayal,
And boyhood dreams of worldly holiness
Fade out at the breaking of dawn!

Out this life we slip, slip to a man-made world,
Existing like instruments with atomic nerves;
We walk on grains of sinking sand,
Living on the security of brittle promises,
Tarnishing truth and lauding vice,
Disgracing the world – our home.

When my friend sees me
He swells and pants like a frog
Because I talk the wisdom of the bush!
He says we from the bush
Do not understand civilized ways
For we tell our women
To keep the hem of their dresses
Below the knee.
We from the bush, my friend insists,
Do not know how to 'enjoy':
When we come to the civilized city,
Like nuns, we stay away from nightclubs
Where women belong to no men
And men belong to no women
And these civilized people
Quarrel and fight like hungry lions!

But, my friend, why do men
With crippled legs, lifeless eyes,
Wooden legs, empty stomachs
Wander about the streets
Of this civilized world?

Teach me, my friend, the trick,
So that my eyes may not
See those whose houses have no walls
But emptiness all around;
Show me the wax you use
To seal your ears
To stop hearing the cry of the hungry;

Teach me the new wisdom
Which tells men
To talk about money and not love,
When they meet women;

Tell your God to convert
Me to the faith of the indifferent,
The faith of those
Who will never listen until
They are shaken with blows.

I speak for the bush:
You speak for the civilized –
Will you hear me?

PARVIN SYAL *The Pot*

I should not have been here,
for I am alien;
They chatter, in a language
that is not my own,
and as I, poor bloke,
try to listen, they laugh,
in a tone that is alien.

I should not have been here,
for I am alien;
Paw-paw, still in the compound,
the grass, dry as of the sun,
dust on the pavement, on my
shoes, and my white pants,
I sit, but am alien.

I should not have been here,
for I am alien;
Teeth being picked, hair brushed,
lips ochred, doom spelt
in many such an application;
I should not have allowed,
the alien arms to circle me.

I should not have been here,
for I am alien;
Head crowned in green,
attired in nothingness, except
ochre, my hands clasped,
feet sore, nettles, sharp,
led to the pot.

I should not have been here,
for I am alien.

[167]

They all pass, they feel and pass,
they stare at me, and poke,
as though I were in a stall,
a stallion, a foal, a mare.
Tribal sheikhs, turbaned, glorious,
their beards reeking with scent,
plumes glistening in the sun,
shekels jingling the rhythm of bidding.
Matrons, spitting tobacco and foul words,
chins pressed against their throats,
bodies bent to the weights of
heavy consciences and sagging breasts.
Horses neighing, riders whipping,
Don Juans bursting into fits of laughter,
Master beseeching, begging, creeping,
to get a fat amount for me.
I stand, erect, a market-piece, as
the Sheikh pats me on my bottom,
I cannot flinch an eye-lid,
or squeak or squeal, but bear.
I feel the stare, am ashamed, but
as my cloth is pulled off,
can only despise the rubied hands,
that feel and press my budding breasts.
Fingers slide across my arms, and
I feel the lust as they crawl
on my naked limbs, attesting me
fit, to draw waters from a well.

They jingle their shekels, they
bid and raise their prices,
flash their rubies, and
take part in my auctioning.
I know what it is to be
defeated and captured in war.

When I came here
it was an intention of mine
to stay, to live and linger.
When I stayed here,
and when my mind
accustomed itself to your sight,
I was asked to leave.

When I packed to leave,
and when in your presence
I bowed for leave-taking,
your eyes shone, a tear
trickled. You wanted me.

Barriers crept up,
thorns lined my paths,
and, as I bled, I
remembered that time,
and urged my movement further.
Tell me, did I surge forward in vain?

I know not the answer –
just a glint as my
guide; is it futile?
Answer, before I stretch
my arms, as I hate
being rejected.

MOHAMED TALIB *The Corpse*

I dreamt about a corpse
Who had come back
To fulfil his hopes
And he said
I've come to gather
The harvest of my deeds and seeds
That I sowed
On my last visit.

I shook hands with a man
Who died the next day
And had never dreamt
Of a Nobel prize
Which to everyone's surprise
Was actually bestowed
Four thousand miles away
Ten minutes before.

I kissed a face in tears
That had mourned the years,
Fed on hopes,
Now hanged dead on ropes;
And daily she postponed her happiness
By crying on purpose
So that she always had
Something to live for.

The corpse fulfils the hopes
The corpse fulfils the hopes.

MOHAMED TALIB *Inanimate Sympathy*

The window shutters shuddering
Saying we told you so
The clouds crouching past
Saying we are truly sorry

The mantel adamant and mute
Tacitly apologizing
Faithfully like a yellow newspaper
Awkwardly.

Don't!
I don't want any bland sympathy
From effeminate candlesticks
Or obsequious chairs.

The titanic trees
Unshakeable and towering:
We are safe and happy;
You should have asked us

Window panes glibly reflecting
Shining like sorry eyes
Compassionate yet quite flat,
Saying we all know

Out!
Get out of my mind
Stop talking to me
Don't sympathize

Burn it . . . kill it . . . slaughter it
And then come and water it

Myself am shared by countries two,
    A fever brought by both;
The hot, the cold, the blaze, the brine,
    Are temperatures of truth.

The one's concerned with supple stream,
    With windings like an alphabet,
An eddy's lip, a phrase, a fish,
    Sentences of liquid;

The other has in roaring water
    Ramifying falls,
A trip of rock, a clap of shine,
    Crocodile and caterwaul.

The one is made of winter's war,
    Snowy siege and dash of flake,
And, inch by inch, in retreat,
    The bugle of bird brakes;

The other seems for summer told
    A fable out of flame,
Trees and spicy fronds and buds
    Forever game.

It is, for such a man as I,
    Chosen not to choose;
I live to love;
    A double muse.

I, too, have lain amongst roses
and danced with the daughter of ghosts
I, too, have followed a story
and sung upon a reed

I, too, have dared my cups
in goblet and in grape
and rocked unreadily homewards
leaning as a lord

I, too, have played with fountains
in asphodel and plain
and wandered to where a ruby
blooded a breeze

I, too, have known how to shiver
in the midnight's darling river
and taken the tree of blossoming dark
to celebrate my heart

I, too, have done my damndest
to kiss and touch and bless
and now I, too, am through with it all
and am simply like the rest

B. TEJANI *In the Orthopaedic Ward*

There in the corner he sits
naked to the waist
the shrunk haunches flattened
against earth.

A hand stretches,
his fingers ambling along
the twisted back-bone,
gingerly tasting the raw-flesh.

Dark face of ape-man
carved from an anthropoid race
scraggy hair of grass-ashen
the liquid eyes
sickled of all intelligence.

He too a man of my race,
my ward,
very much the first in the queue
the recognition of which
gleams in his eye.

Nothing but the stillness
of the snow
and an ageless majesty
matched
by those enduring horizons
that bridge the heights
of you and me.

The phosphorescent sun
gliding from the dark cloud
under us
shone a brief once
while we lay
retching in the rarefied air.

No great triumph in the soul
of those
twenty thousand agonied steps
upwards, always onward.
Only anguish of an ending –
the vacuumed intestines
shivering at another onslaught of
mountain sickness.

An ice-axe prod
in the back
and with it
the terrible thought
of the awful retreat
down the cold slopes
of possible deaths;
dumb eyes and feet

lit by a single
tireless search
for slumber
which is as far away from us
as we from the plains.

Only when
the nightmare is over
I shall remember
the dogged voice of
conscience
self-pity warring with will
of the brown body
to keep up
with the black flesh
forging ahead
on the way
to Kilimanjaro.

With savannas on our left
and on our right
the white-ribbed road
stretching to the sky
we felt the master
of those alluvial plains
untrod by man.

The car's boom
was our lonely space-flight
its forward thrusting power
our stream line
its dust-storm
our rocket-fuel.

When suddenly with a jolt
we came back to earth
as he stood
translucent, sun-muscle coated
with arched neck
and thick nostrils
quicksilver quivering,
that wild horse of Serengeti.

This was his kingdom,
the arid peace of the plains his,
the merged mountain and sky
and the white-ribbed road
where he stood square
with gun-powder feet.

[178]

At howl of the machine toot,
lonely as a walk in space
he exploded convulsively
feet limbs and body
boosting each other
and rose
rose.

And my God!
came straight at us
his dark hooves
kniving the air,
the haunches and belly
fighting a fierce wild Medea.

And sailed clean
over the manned machine
grazing raucously with
a black claw
the top
that dented to his supremacy.

The great thumbs stirred
Shivered and pressed a button,
Giant bells rang
In a long thunderous boom,
The tiny death words became
Stronger and more evil,
The great immortality ended in
And echoless endless mortality;
where the night is still
A soft moonlight ivory,
There lies the grave of God with
An epitaph inscribed in
Priceless wood.

The woman I married
Is an out-right bone-shaker.
For a full decade
She had banged a typewriter
And now in substitution
Bangs the crockery
Until my house sounds like a factory.

The noise keeps her sane,
They say.

Bruised face,
Hacked ribs,
Intestines frantically harrowed out
By machine-dislocated men
Sweating in subterranean cells
Deep as the grave of mankind –
The projected havoc
Of the frenzy in human blood.

TIMOTHY WANGUSA *A Strange Wind*

A strange wind is blowing, dust fills our eyes:
We turn and walk the unintended way.
We press our sore eyes and reopen them
To expanded horizons, to a new day!
The narrow circle of our cherished experience breaks,
Our trusted gods dissolve and ghosts vanish,
Disembodied voices announce world news,
We see the hidden side of the moon,
The dead man's eye transfers to the living,
The atom splits and the songbird croaks,
Economics opposes Charity,
Law protects wizards and forbids justice,
The small nation shouts, and the big one brags,
Futile raids cease and global wars commence,
And the rude son strikes the father – a sword!

By the ashes of Sodom
And of Gomorrah, Lord,
Behold me weeping, by
The ashes of men
Once nimbler than he-goat.

Not a breath
Not a trace
Where at threshold hands itched
Beyond sacrifice to touch the
Origin of flame.

Then at God-time
The terror-pelt
And I
Suddenly
On legs of feather
Running and running and
Beating the air
Gaze fixed on
Demented shadow
Running and
Beating the air
While at my back
The noise of doom
Hissing and wailing.

And amid the tumult, O God,
The costly halt of inquiring feet.

And this, Lord, the outline
This the beloved face that

[184]

Thenceforth I have dreaded and
Encountered in all my dreams;
The pained look forever piercing,
Forever probing and doubting the
Obedience and love –
This the God-planted pillar
In this singed valley to proclaim
The eternity
Of the backward glance.

    God the Terror
    God the Favour
At whose voice what earth-melting!
By whose hand what mountain safety!
    God the Moulder
    God the Remover
What wonder will not spring at thy bidding?
What stones not happily turn to flesh?

Dresses and trousers
On God-like rock.

When with prophetic eye I peer into the future
I see that I shall perish upon this road
Driving men that I do not know.
This metallic monster that now I dictate,
This docile elaborate horse,
That in silence seems to simmer and strain,
Shall surely revolt some tempting day.
Thus I shall die; not that I care
For any man's journey,
Nor for proprietor's gain,
Nor yet for love of my own.
Not for these do I attempt the forbidden limits,
For these defy the traffic-man and the cold cell,
Risking everything for the little little more.
They shall say, I know, who pick up my bones,
'Poor chap, another victim to the ruthless machine' –
Concealing my blood under the metal.

BIOGRAPHICAL NOTES

JARED ANGIRA is Editor of *Busara*. He has published *Juices* (EAPH 1970), and a forthcoming book of poems, *Silent Voices*, is to be published by Heinemann. He is at present studying for a B. Com. at the University of East Africa and hopes to graduate in 1971. He says: 'Karl Max is my teacher; Pablo Neruda my class prefect (when I am in a class-room) and my captain (when I am on the battlefield). Although I am *no longer at ease* here, I have been cautioned to contain my malady without bitterness. I have to confront the *world without end* and see how to endure all in the spirit of forgetting all past and present bad things.'

PETER ANYANG'-NYONG'O was educated at Ndiru Primary School, Alliance High School and Makerere, where he graduates in 1971. His active interest in drama resulted in leading parts in several productions at Alliance High School and participation in the 1969 Makerere Travelling Theatre. He has had occasional poems published in the press; was Schools Drama Critic for *The Daily Nation* 1967–69; and has been a script writer and broadcaster in programmes in history and English for the Schools Broadcasting Division of the Voice of Kenya since 1965.

HENRY BARLOW is 42 years old, married, with five children. He was educated at King's College, Budo (1936–48); Makerere University, Kampala (1949–53); and he spent one academic year at Oxford in 1959–60. Immediately after leaving Makerere he joined the Civil Service as a Co-operative Officer, and went through the ranks until 1964 when he was appointed Permanent Secretary. He has now been seconded from the Civil Service and is Chairman of Lint Marketing Board. He has published two poems in a collection called *Drum Beat* under the name of Y. S. Chemba and a further two poems in *Zuka*.

[187]

He is not a regular writer and he says that he writes either to relieve himself of some strong feeling or to explore the feeling.

A.S. BUKENYA was born in Masaka, Uganda in February 1944. After secondary school in Kampala, he joined the University of Dar es Salaam in Tanzania, where he read Literature, Linguistics, and French. He was a founder co-editor of *Darlite*, the University's literary journal, and was the first student in the University's history to graduate with a First Class Honours degree, in March 1968. He took an M.A. degree in Traditional African Literature at Makerere University, Kampala, where he now lectures in Literature. He has published a one-act play in *Short East African Plays in English*, poems in *Just A Moment, God,* and a handbook on public speech in Luganda, his mother tongue. His first novel, *The People's Bachelor*, was published in Nairobi in February 1971.

JOHN BUTLER studied for his degree in English while teaching full-time in England. He came to Uganda in 1959 as Headmaster of Lubiri Secondary School in Kampala, one of the very first day secondary schools in Uganda to carry students through to school certificate. Later he was founder Headmaster of the first secondary school in Karamoja. He is currently tutor in English at the National Teachers' College. He has published a number of poems and prose writings in *Transition* and elsewhere.

MURRAY CARLIN was born in Johannesburg, South Africa. He was educated at St John's College, Johannesburg, Rhodes University, and Emmanuel College, Cambridge. He fought as a rifleman in the Libyan Campaign of the Second World War; was taken prisoner after the fall of Tobruk, and suffered, while under the power of Hitler, various dangers and deprivations. He is a widower; the father of three daughters and one son; a teacher by profession, a poet in aspiration.

JIM CHAPLIN was Director of Monuments in Uganda when he was knocked down and killed in Kampala in March 1967. He was well known to many young writers in East Africa and put much of his own enthusiasm and interest into writing and discussing poetry.

A. R. CLIFF-LUBWA was born in Gulu, Northern Uganda, and did his primary education in Kitgum, East Acholi, where his father was a Medical Assistant. He then went to Sir Samuel Baker School, Gulu, before going on to do a Diploma in Education. He is now teaching English at St. Charles Lwanga College, Koboko Senior Secondary School. His short collection, *The Beloved and Other Poems*, is being published by the East African Publishing House, Nairobi, and he is preparing another collection at the moment. Some of his poems, including *The Beloved*, have been broadcast on B.B.C. London.

SAROJ DATTA was born in Kampala, Uganda. She spent her childhood in East Africa, except for several long visits to India, the land of her parents. In December 1968 her family settled in Britain; she is at the time of going to press reading English and Philosophy at the University of Glasgow.

SHEIKHA A. EL-MISKERY, daughter of the Sheikha of

[189]

Al-Alaya, Oman, was born 10th October, 1944, in Ibra the capital city. Her childhood years were spent in the Middle East and East Africa, and she graduated with honours in English Literature from Makerere University in 1967. She began writing early on, but did not publish anything until her college days. Since that time her poetry has appeared in various publications and has been broadcast in several countries. She is currently pursuing graduate studies in America.

LABAN ERAPU is a Makerere graduate taking an M.Litt. course in Afro-Caribbean Literature in Edinburgh University when this publication went to press. While at Makerere he also wrote one-act plays and his first novel, *Restless Feet*. His plays were performed in Makerere (where he was a member of the Travelling Theatre) and they have been broadcast over Radio Uganda. He has also featured on the B.B.C. African Service where his writing has been read and discussed on the 'Writers Club' programmes. As an undergraduate he was chief editor of the *Makererean*, the university paper, for a year, and he has also worked on a national newspaper.

DAVID GILL was born in Chislehurst, Kent, in 1934. He attended the local grammar school and later read German at University College, London. Eighteen months of making Dunlop tyres convinced him that he did not wish to be a deck-hand, let alone a Captain of Industry: he turned, therefore, to teaching. He went with his family to Uganda in 1962 to teach at Nyakasura School, just in time to see the advent of Independence. Apart from teaching English he learnt something about Ugandan music, wrote poems, and dug a fish-pond in the nearby swamp with his long-suffering students. Still in touch with Uganda, he now lives with his wife and three children in Oxford. *Men Without Evenings*, his first volume of verse, was followed in 1969 by *The Pagoda and Other Poems*.

CRISPIN HAULI was born in 1945 at Ilela Manda. He is the second son of a missionary teacher. He graduated from the University of East Africa at Dar es Salaam in 1970 with a degree in Education, Economics, and Literature. He is a keen athlete and writer. A number of his short plays, stories, and poems have appeared in *Darlite*. Some of his poems written in Swahili, *Mashiri Tasa*, have attracted attention. He is now a tutor at Dar es Salaam College of National Education, where he has worked since his graduation.

SABITI KABUSHENGA was born to Justin Faith and George William Kabushenga in the year 1942 on a Sunday, hence the name Sabiti. His childhood was neither colourful nor undistinguished and he is the eldest of eleven sisters and brothers. He was educated at Nyamiyaga Church School, Rwere Church School, Kigezi High School, Nyakatale Boys Primary School, Kinyasano Junior Secondary School, Kigezi High School again, Kigezi College Butokene, Glastonbury High School, Connecticut, U.S.A., Makerere College School, and Makerere University College, then the University of East Africa. There was nothing throughout his education to indicate that he would be a writer; indeed one of his weakest points in English was his inability to appreciate poetry. When he started writing poetry in 1967 he realized that instead of using the most natural way of writing, that is in verse, people laboured to produce chapters of boring prose. He thinks that the ability to speculate or penetrate into things or even the ability to express oneself in verse does not entitle one to tell human beings what they ought not to do and what they ought to see.

For the present, therefore, he has settled down to doing what other human beings do. He has a job and earns his daily bread.

WILLIAM KAMERA was born at Mwika Moshi, Kiliman-jaro, Tanzania, on 18th April, 1942. He entered Ilboru Secondary School in Arusha where he studied for his Cambridge School Certificates. In 1965 he entered the University of East Africa at Dar es Salaam and graduated in 1969 with an upper second class Honours Degree in Literature, Linguistics, and Education. While at college, he was a member of the Literature Panel of the Ministry of Education, and after obtaining his degree he was appointed Tutorial Assistant in the Department of Literature at Dar es Salaam. He started graduate studies in English at Cornell in the fall of 1969. He is married and has two children. In 1964 he won the First Prize in a Poetry Competition organized by the East African Literature Bureau and sponsored by the Rockefeller Foundation. He has also been editor of *Darlite*, the student magazine at the University College, and a member of the University Theatre Group. Some of his poems have appeared in *Transition*.

JONATHAN KARIARIA is an editor with Oxford University Press in Nairobi. He has published many short stories and poems, in particular in *Zuka*.

JOSEPH KARIUKI was born in 1931. He attended the Kenya Institute of Administration, and then spent a year with the Economic Commission for Africa as the chief of their Training Unit, before being appointed Director-General of CAFRAD towards the end of 1969. He confesses that his literary activities have subsided considerably since he went into public administration for the simple reason that his position as an administrative head has absorbed all his energies and left him too tired to be creative in a literary sense.

AMIN KASSAM was born in Mombasa on 19th November, 1948. He began writing poetry at the age of eighteen and since then he has had his work published in several East African magazines. He has also been anthologized in *Drum Beat*. In addition, his poetry has been broadcast over Radio Uganda, Voice of Kenya, and the B.B.C. Amin also writes short stories which have appeared in *Busara* (of which he was once assistant editor), and the *Journal of the New African Literature and the Arts*.

YUSUF O. KASSAM is a Tanzanian, born in Tanzania in 1943. He obtained his B.A. in English and History from Maker- ere University College, Kampala, in 1966. In 1967 he obtained a post-graduate Diploma in Education from the same Univer- sity. From 1967 to 1969 he taught at Mzumbe Government Boys' Secondary School, Morogoro. In January 1970 he joined the Institute of Adult Education, University of Dar es Salaam, where he works as an Assistant Resident Tutor. Wordsworth's philosophy on poetry, and poetry itself, which he had to study for his H.S.C., began his interest in poetry, and it was in 1964 that he first began to write his own. His poems have been published in different anthologies such as *Young Commonwealth Poets '65* (Heinemann) and *New Voices of the Commonwealth* (Evans Brothers). They have also been published in various journals, magazines, and newspapers, such as *East Africa Journal*, *Penpoint*, *The People*, etc. Some of his poems have also been broadcast and discussed over the B.B.C. African Service. In 1965 he won a poetry prize in a competition organized by the Cardiff Commonwealth Arts Festival.

BIOGRAPHICAL NOTES

TABAN LO LIYONG, one of the most stimulating figures in East African writing, was born in Uganda in 1938. He was the first African to receive a Master of Fine Arts degree from the famous Writers Workshop of the University of Iowa. He has already published two highly individual books in the African Writers Series, *Fixions* (AWS 69), a collection of stories, and *Eating Chiefs* (AWS 74), a personal transmutation of Lwo poetry. In 1971 a new collection entitled *Frantz Fanon's Uneven Ribs: Poems, More & More* (AWS 90) was published. He has also published a collection of literary criticism, *The Last Word* (EAPH). After his return to East Africa in 1968 he was in the Cultural Division of the Institute for Development Studies at the University of Nairobi, working on research into Lwo and Masai literature. He is now a lecturer in English in the Literature Department.

STEPHEN LUBEGA is a first year student of Literature at Makerere University, Kampala. He was born in 1945 in Masaka District, Uganda, and received his secondary education at Bukalasa Seminary and later joined the National Teachers' College, Kyambogo, where he obtained a Diploma in teaching in 1967. Since then he has been teaching English in secondary schools. He was the first editor of *Student Lines*, a literary magazine of the National Teachers' College. Some of his writings have appeared in East African magazines like *Zuka* and *Flamingo*, and a number of his poems have been heard over the B.B.C. African Service.

JOHN S. MBITI was educated at Makerere, in the United States, and in Britain. His academic interests are in religion and philosophy, and African oral literature and he writes on these subjects. Published books and articles are innumerable, including *Akamba Stories* (1966), *African Religions and Philosophy* (1969),

Poems of Nature and Faith (1969), *Concepts of God in Africa* (1970), *New Testament Eschatology in an African Background* (1970), etc. He is Professor of Religious Studies and Head of the Department of Religious Studies and Philosophy, Makerere University Kampala. He is married, with two children.

ROSE MBOWA. Educated at Kibuye Primary School, Buloba Primary School, Gayaza High School, Makerere University College and Leeds University; was born at Kabale in Uganda in 1943; has worked as a broadcaster for Radio Uganda and is at the moment working as a tutor in drama at Makerere University, Kampala.

ALEXANDER MUIGAI attended Dr. Aggrey Primary School, then Pumwani Secondary School, where in his fourth year he was head boy. He then proceeded to Nairobi School where he sat for A levels in 1969. His hobbies include motor cycling, mountaineering, swimming, photography and drawing. He writes poetry as a means of recording feelings, experiences, and observations. He is now at Rugby School, England, where he went in January 1970, and he hopes to study Zoology at College.

PAUL MUKASA-SSALI was born in 1946. He attended Busoga College, Mwiri, Makerere College School, and Makerere University where he graduated in English Honours in 1970. He won the Taylor Essay Prize (1964), the Brooke Bond Tea Essay Prize (1964), and the Makerere University Exhibition Prize (1970). He edited one issue of *Penpoint* during 1970.

MAGEMESO NAMUNGALU was born on 19th January,

BIOGRAPHICAL NOTES

1948. He was educated at Iganga, Kiyunga Junior School, and
the Senior Secondary School, Jinja. He did his Cambridge
School Certificate in eleven years instead of the usual twelve.
His interest in writing dates from when he first knew of writing.
He met Professor D. J. Cook in 1968, to whom he is whole-
heartedly indebted for his generous help. His poems have been
read on Radio Uganda and his favourite poets are Okot,
Shakespeare, D. H. Lawrence, and Houseman.

STELLA NGATHO is doing A levels in Geography, Art,
and Literature at Kenya High School.

VICTOR NGWABE, son of Yoronimu Ngwabe, comes from
Eastern Uganda, Bukedi District. He was born in 1941 in a
small village in southern Bukedi where his parents still live.
Victor had his initial primary school education in Mission
schools, and was forced to stop schooling for some years due to
lack of school fees. Later he studied at St. Peter's College,
Tororo; Teso College, Aloet; and Makerere University,
Kampala, where he graduated in March 1970 with B.A.
honours in Literature.

RICHARD NTIRU was born in 1946, near Kisoro, South
West Uganda. He attended Secondary School at Ntare School,
Mbarara where he became interested in play acting and verse
sketching. In 1968 he entered Makerere University's Depart-
ment of Literature where he edited the Campus Newspaper,
Makererean, organized the 1969 Makerere Arts Festival,
participated in the renowned Makerere Travelling Theatre,
and edited the Campus Journal of Creative Writing, *Penpoint*.
Besides a radio play and a few stories, he has contributed

[196]

poems to East African magazines, a selection of which will soon be brought out by the East African Publishing House.

BENEDICT ONYANGO OGUTU was educated at St Mary's School, Yala, north of Kisumu. He works for the East African Publishing House, for whom he tours East Africa 'talking books' to the people. His book of Luo heritage, *Keep My Words*, will appear soon. He has published poetry in various East African magazines.

OKELLO OCULI was born in 1942 and comes from Lang'o, Uganda. He has published a novel, *Prostitute*, and also *Orphan*, a long poem. He is widely recognized as one of the most explosive figures on the contemporary literary scene in East Africa.

OKOT P'BITEK is working in the Extra-Mural Department of Nairobi University. He was born in Gulu, Northern Uganda, in 1931, and was educated at Gulu High School and King's College, Budo. Okot has played football for Uganda. He read Education at Bristol, Law at Aberystwyth, and Social Anthropology at Oxford. He has lectured at Makerere and in the U.S.A., and has been Director of the National Theatre, Kampala. He founded the Gulu Festival. In 1953 he published a Lwo novel; and has had poems and articles in several of the journals which appear in East Africa. Okot p'Bitek is best known for his two long poems, *Song of Lawino* and *Song of Ocol*, published by the East African Publishing House.

OPINYA H. W. OKOTH-OGENDO, LL.B. (E.A.), formerly

[197]

of the University College, Dar es Salaam; and Special Assistant Lecturer in the Department of Law and Jurisprudence, Faculty of Law, University of Nairobi. He is at presant Winter Williams Student at Wadham College, Oxford. Author of *The Dancing Maniac* in *Just a Moment, God* (E. A. L. B. 1970), and regular contributor in *Ghala, Busara* and *Darlite*. Also author of several legal essays in *Journal of Denning Law Society* (University of Dar es Salaam publication).

MARJORIE OLUDHE-MAOGOYE was born in England in 1928 and went to Kenya in 1954 with C. M. S. Bookshop. She has a London M.A. in English and has edited some Lwo Historical Texts. Married to a Lwo medical man, she has four children.

CHARLES OWOUR is 23. He did his A levels in 1968 at Strathmore College, Nairobi and has since been travelling.and studying with the Friends World Institute.

DAVID RUBADIRI. Born in 1930 in Malawi. Went to school at King's College, Budo; then to the Universities of Makerere, Bristol, and Cambridge. His main interest has always been in literature and writing. He is now teaching literature at Makerere University, Kampala.

JOHN RUGANDA was born in 1941 in Fort Portal, Uganda. He was educated at St. Leo's College and Ntare School before going to read English Honours at Makerere University. He now works with Oxford University Press as Editorial and Sales Representative in Uganda.

[198]

PROSCOVIA RWAKYAKA has recently spent a year in New York on an M.A. programme at Teachers College, Colombia University. She has returned to Tororo Girls' School and continues teaching English. She started teaching at Tororo in May 1967 immediately after she left Makerere University, Kampala. In her early years she went to Kyebambe Girls School and Gayaza High School. Her home and her parents are in Fort Portal but she has spent little time there.

NUWA SENTONGO born 3rd November, 1942, went to Kungu Primary School, Makerere College School, Makerere University College and Indiana University. He is currently a lecturer at Makerere University, Kampala.

JAGJIT SINGH. A Ugandan, born in 1949, went to Senior Secondary School, Kololo, where he was awarded a Gold Medal for obtaining four distinctions in A levels in 1969: he is now reading Literature at the School of African and Asian Studies at the University of Sussex, and hopes eventually to be a film scriptwriter or a University Lecturer but above all to *write* the agony and the ecstasy of being alive. First felt an awareness of the creative spirit at the age of twelve after reading a simplified version of R. L. Stevenson's *Kidnapped*. He pub-lised his first poem at 16, worked for *The People* and *Flamingo* at 18, and has had stories and poems published in the *East Africa Journal*.

JOHN SSEMUWANGA was born near Kampala, and he received his primary and secondary education in missionary schools. His interest in poetry originated from the fascinating and captivating charm he found in nursery rhymes. Partly

[199]

because of his background, and partly because of the missionary influence at school, he acquired a religious attitude in his outlook on life which never diminished. It is perhaps because of this ingrained fervour that most of his poems, while not strictly religious, tend to invoke some kind of soul-searching plea. His greatest literary ambition is to write a novel some day.

EVERETT STANDA was born and educated in Mahanga village of Western Province, Kenya. Writing is a hobby he finds most satisfying and recreative. It is also a way in which he effects the living dialogue between society, people, and himself. He now works in the National Christian Council's Communications Office, Nairobi.

PARVIN SYAL, born in December 1947, was launched into poetry by his father's encouragement at the age of ten. He wrote poetry for many competitions and was awarded prizes on numerous occasions. Apart from being a poet, writing both in English and Hindi, he has always been a debating enthusiast, and was responsible for initiating and organizing the 'Upper Hill Schools', Nairobi Inter-schools' Debating Tournament. Recently, his hitherto unpublished play, *Through a Hand-cuff*, attained third position in the play competition organized by the Department of English, University of Nairobi. Although he is at present a medical student at Nairobi University, he finds time to read a lot.

MOHAMED TALIB was born in Mombasa on 4th February, 1947. Prior to his university education, he was more interested in biology than literature. However, his family background led him to more religious and literary pursuits, and he eventually ended up more interested in the arts. In 1969 he obtained his

B.A. Honours Degree in Literature. He has been doing free-lance writing since then, and his main preoccupation has been the futility of man's existence enclosed by space and time. He has immense faith in the concept of life after death, but considers it important for man to identify himself culturally and spiritually before dying.

BARRY TAYLOR has been teaching in Uganda for some years. His most recent publication is a verse novel, *The Rhyme of Francis Fall*, Outposts, 1970.

B. TEJANI was born on the slopes of Kilimanjaro. He read Literature at Makerere and Philosophy at Cambridge. He has published a book of protest on India called *The Rape of Literature*, and also written for most of the East African magazines and newspapers. He lectures at the University of Nairobi. His novel *Day After Tomorrow* will be published by the Literature Bureau in 1971.

HUBERT TEMBA was born in Moshi, Tanzania in November 1951. He received some of his education at Mawenzi Secondary School, Moshi from 1966 to 1969, and is now studying for his H.S.C. which he hopes to sit in 1971. For some time now he has been concentrating on poetry writing but he also devotes time to writing prose and he is a keen music lover.

EDWIN WAIYAKI was born in 1939 and is the thirteenth child of a family of sixteen. After senior schooling at Thika High School he continued his studies in Paris.

[201]

TIMOTHY WANGUSA was born in Bugisu District, Uganda, in 1942. Read English at Makerere University College and at the University of Leeds before returning to Makerere in 1969 as a Tutorial Fellow. Some of his poetry has appeared in *East Africa Journal*, and in *New Voices of the Commonwealth*, edited by Howard Sergent.

DAVID COOK was a schoolteacher in England for many years and took two internal part-time degrees from the University of London. He taught for five years in the University of Southampton before moving permanently to Makerere in 1962 where he became Head of the Department of Literature in 1967. Has published major editions of seventeenth century plays, and a volume on the background to Elizabethan/Jacobean drama, as well as numerous articles – in particular on drama and education. He launched the Makerere Travelling Theatre in 1965. He edited the first published volume of East African prose, and co-edited a book of East African plays.

INDEX OF FIRST LINES

A cockerel crows, 132

After I have communed with them, 12

After the parents have gone to burn the houses of the parents below, 45

A leopard lives in a Muu tree, 64

A limping little cupid of farce, 112

Alone in the vast forest of elders, 111

A stranger's smile captures my untutored heart, 164

A strange wind is blowing, dust fills our eyes, 183

At dusk, mother, 143

Atieno washes dishes, 134

Brown, proud and flawless, 43

Bruised face, 182

By the ashes of Sodom, 184

By this well, 20

Crack the glass, 36

Dawn is breaking, 123

Dead on my palm, 35

Dry-season dust-tails dogged the cars along, 47

For sixty years or more the mission church, 46

Frisk me out, dear, 154

Gloria Bishop, 88

Greet for me the son of Karanja, 66

Hear, hear this my poem, 26

HEAVENSGATE, 140

Here I sit with every mortal gadget round me, 44

He was buried without a coffin, 4

I am a crucified thief, 94

I beg you, 40

I confess ive never met a chinese who looks old, 84

I desired her, 139

I dreamt about a corpse, 171

I envied his being Negro, 28

If you should take my child Lord, 63

I go to my old father, 124

I have walked, 138

I hear sweet voice and my heart beats, 120

I'll put aside my hoe, 102

I love you, my gentle one, 23

I love you my Lord, 26

In the pulpit he swayed and turned, 147

Irreconcilable love and pity. 93

I see a road, 136

I should not have been here, 167

Is this the junction he meant?, **150**

It is the sweet death, **146**

It was that memorable night when I heard it, **78**

I, too, have lain amongst roses, **174**

Lapobo, **34**

Let not your grinning ads lure me, **96**

Let us not lie to ourselves, **29**

Marry me, **86**

Men of the milder zone, you find, **31**

Mr. Gwentamu submits, **54**

My man is gone away to serve, **6**

Myself am shared by countries two, **173**

Never has the death of a poet, **92**

Nothing breaks the silence of sleep's territory, **122**

Nothing but the stillness, **176**

Nothing makes me madder, **90**

Now when into the far past I pry, **148**

Old men wait at the stop, **76**

'Old soldiers never die', **140**

O Lord Make Haste to Help Me, **2**

Only those, **116**

On the beach, on the coast, **27**

Oo, from which wing do you come? **108**

Path-let ... leaving home, leading out, **109**

Pauper, pauper, craning your eyes, **114**

People walk, **80**

Putting butter on a slice, and in the pan rice, **24**

Sitting on a stool outside his mud hut, **77**

Some people fear death, **160**

Some urgency imprisoned among the drums, **30**

Somewhere in the distance church bells are chiming, **162**

That chloroform sleep, **8**

The distance we've travelled together is short, **62**

The dog in Kivulu, **22**

The drum beats, **81**

The field was full of bruised babies, **67**

The great thumbs stirred, **180**

The kraal fence, **110**
The leaves are withered, **60**
The maize will grow, **1**
The monotonous tap of the blacksmiths' sounds, **33**
The past has boiled itself over, **156**
There in the corner he sits, **175**
There's a strong wind that breaks on Katebo Port, **104**
There she lay in a pool of blood, **107**
There she was on the Nile, puffing, **149**
The rising sun on a Sunday morning, **105**
The sun set, night came, and everything was dark, **82**
The weak scattered rays of yellow sun, **95**
The window shutters shuddering, **172**
The Witch Tree, **142**
The woman I married, **181**
They all pass, they feel and pass, **168**
They are rooted here. Their tenuous life, **48**
They drive me along, **49**
They no longer sleep, **72**
They sowed and watered, **130**
Those eyes!, **16**
Today I did my share, **14**
Towers of strength, **137**

Under Abraham's vacant eyes, **73**
Under warm sunshine, **83**
Unthinking of kids she could be carrying, **152**
Up on a hill it stood immovable, **100**

Village grown large, **74**
Virgine Madre, **118**

Warm scent, **75**
Was this where I came staggering?, **32**
We are the solitary street travellers, **99**
We are tired of waiting for another war, **98**
We lived long time ago, **50**
What formless forms do you sense, **161**
When dogs encounter, **37**
When he was here, **38**
When I came here, **170**
When I was young mother told me to shut up, **91**
When my friend sees me, **165**
When with prophetic eye I peer into the future, **186**
When you come, dear friend, **106**
When you have whispered it in my cocked ear, **113**

When you left, **70**

With dazzling eyes: sweet poison in teeth, **101**

With savannas on our left, **178**

Worms crawling, Worms crawling, **10**

You dragged me, **71**

Your nails are black with dirt, brother, **18**

Yours were the eyes that wouldn't wander, **39**

You've seen that heap of rags, **42**